KNOWLEDGE THROUGH DIRECT COGNITION

by Julian Hamer

© All rights reserved. No part of this publication may be reproduced without the prior permission of the author.
Revised Edition, 2020

This book is dedicated to my beautiful wife Ellen for her patience, support and encouragement.

KNOWLEDGE THROUGH DIRECT COGNITION

The Human, Conscious Individuality and Immediately Experienced Reality

by Julian Hamer

TABLE OF CONTENTS

1. OVERVIEW: Authenticity and the Superficial p3
2. DIRECT, EXPERIENTIAL COGNITION: Uninhibited, Cognitive Encounter through the mind-self p.15
3. PHYSICAL APPEARANCES: The Restricted Mentality of the Materialist p.23
4. INCORPOREAL REALITY: The Folly of the Materialistic Denial of the Intangible p.35
5. THE HUMAN MIND-SELF: Recognition of Essential Identity of the Human Being p.43
6. REALITY, DIRECT EXPERIENCED: Knowledge of the Real Through Immediate Cognition p.51
7. TRUE OR FALSE – REAL AND UNREAL: The Importance of the Distinction Between these Terms p.55
8. THE PERSPECTIVE OF THE MIND-SELF: The Real and Authentic Recognizes its Own Nature p.61
9. KNOWLEDGE AND THE MIND-SELF: Exploration of the Human Capacity of Direct Cognition p.71
10. THE INTRINSIC NATURE: The Essential, Qualitative Reality Explored p.77
11. THE AUTHORITY OF THE HUMAN MIND-SELF: Mind-Self Cognition Applied to Nature p.91
12. OPEN-MINDED OBSERVATION: The Avian Concept p.103
13. FROM UNDEFINED TO SPECIFIC: The Manner Whereby an Overall, Governing Principle is Variously Interpreted p.113
14. THE ESSENTIAL IDENTITY: Superficial Properties and Qualitative, Intrinsic Significance p.121
15. LIFEFORMS: Viable Organic Organization and the Agencies of Life p.129
16. THE IDEAL CONCEPT: The Realization of the Archetype p.137
17. A QUALITATIVE EXAMINATION: Sunlight, Color and Darkness p.143
18. THE NATURE AND MANNER WHEREBY A PHENOMENON IS EXPRESSED: Observations from the Perspective of the Immediate Experience p.159
19. THE HUMAN CAPACITY OF DIRECT COGNITION: Human, Conscious Individuality p.169
20. THE IMMEDIATE EXPERIENCE OF REALITY: With Reference to the Works of Rene Descartes p.175
21. ARTICULATING INTANGIBLE REALITIES: Art as the Language of Quintessential Knowledge p.201
CONCLUSION p.209
Other Books by the same author p217

Introduction

We are very familiar with conventional thinking whereby we associate one thing with our memory concerning another and figure out thereby what a new phenomenon must be. However, this process never arrives at the definitive identity of an object. It merely deals with the affiliation of superficial properties. This is normally sufficiently adequate but, if we wish to know the intrinsic nature of the existence of something, we much apply a different practice of cognition altogether.

We name phenomena and, by the activity of association, we imagine that we know what they are. We further qualify our assessment through reasoning. However, intellectual activity is by its very nature an indirect approach because rationale sorts information but it cannot experience anything directly. It does not lead to consummate knowledge concerning the identity of something but only to a calculated evaluation.

Fortunately, the human being is endowed with an inherent faculty of cognition whereby a phenomenon may be experienced directly and thereby known for what it actually and authentically is. Thereby, the practice of immediate cognition provides knowledge of the intrinsic identities and essential nature of things that are otherwise obscured.

This latent, experiential capacity of thinking requires the exclusive attention of the human, essential identity towards a phenomenon of interest. The inherent identity of the phenomenon is thereby experienced immediately as insightful knowledge because the essential distinction of the human being has the capacity to recognize the intrinsic reality of the object.

The human, quintessential identity is the conscious individuality. Through direct encounter the human, elementary singularity is able to know a thing profoundly for what it is because the corresponding engagement between an observer and the phenomenon is essential.

Reasoning calculates and enables a phenomenon to be known for how it works and what it is for but if the nature of the essential existence of a thing is sought then immediate cognition through the human, conscious individuality is the only viable recourse. Everyone possesses the inherent faculty of direct cognition as an aspect of their essential constitution. Thereby, the human, essential singularity is able to experience itself and finds that it exists as a unique and inviolate entity. Accordingly, through direct, experiential engagement the human quintessence is able to discover the intrinsic nature of the existence of all phenomena because it is able to immediately discern other similarly essential significances.

1. OVERVIEW
Authenticity and the Superficial

As human beings we possess the inherent capacity to identify a thing in terms of its intangible, intrinsic significance and not merely by its superficial appearance. But we imagine we can tell at a glance what an object is because we compare it to things we have seen before and match it to circumstances that we already know. However, there is more to something than can be discovered through its obvious appearance or by an analytical scrutiny of its blatant, physical properties. If we wish to discover the authentic identity and what a thing intrinsically is and not merely what it physically appears to be, we must engage it originally. That is to say, the direct experience of a phenomenon must remain uninfluenced by what we think we know concerning it and our by our typical process of evaluation. When we wish to discover the intrinsic identity, an object of interest can be known only through an immediate and uninhibited encounter.

In order to recognize the essential identity of a thing and to discover its imperative condition of existence we cannot allow our direct experience to be deflected by preconceived notions concerning it. We need to avoid assessing it through the various associations retrieved from our memory or through sentiment, and we must overlook the habitual tendency towards superficial evaluation. We are trying to discover the authentic identity which requires an original experience untainted by our conventional practices of interpretation.

The authentic identity of a phenomenon exists

independently of the physical appearance. It is intrinsic and, as such, it cannot be found upon the basis of our own ideas pre-established upon the superficial semblance, nor through deduction. Intrinsic particularity is only discovered when the phenomenon is confronted directly and uniquely.

The intangible significance of something is not usually considered of significant merit by conventional wisdom because it is a physically elusive qualification of the physical condition. However, the human capacity of direct engagement differs from intellectual and felling-sentient appraisal through the straightforward, experiential nature of the correspondence. The irony is that while the intangible significance of something is denied value in physical terms, it is nonetheless experienced constantly throughout everyday life. Thus, the determined materialist marginalizes the merit of the qualitative modification of physical conditions and insists upon an oblique, abstract assessment of life that excludes mitigating influences.

For example, when two strangers meet, their first impressions are of their outward and superficial appearances. Initially, they evaluate one another upon that basis. But neither would suggest that the other consist merely of those superficial properties. However, conventionally, that is exactly what we do when we consider the phenomenal world. We observe superficially and consider the appearance as if it were the actual identity.

The authenticity of a person or thing can be determined only through direct engagement with the essential identity. It cannot be calculated intellectually because the actual identity is unrecognizable within the physical parameters and remains unconfirmed by a superficial encounter. Everything has an essential pertinence that is more significant than the concepts retrieved from our memories and of greater profoundness than the obvious semblance.

While the essential cannot be determined in the conventional, cognitive manner and remains beyond the scope and range of deduction, it can become known through direct cognition. Direct cognition is a meeting with a phenomenon without preconception. It is more astute than the usual cerebral activities of association and interpretation or through the examination of physical properties whereby one tries to deduce what something is by an analysis of its parts. Similarly, sentiment and speculation need to be restrained in order that the encounter remains original. Direct cognition is experiential and requires that conventional thinking practices be temporarily suspended in order that they do not detract from the immediacy of the engagement.

When we refrain from comparing something to prior reminiscences and feelings, and postpone trying to figure out what something is, then the observer who remains is not a faculty but our own authentic identity. It is from the essential perspective and through the agency of our own intrinsic person that the primary existence of someone else or of a phenomenon becomes discernible.

The first experience of direct cognition is almost overwhelming because it is unusual to discern the intrinsic significance of things. Formally, we thought in terms of abstract concepts or sentiment, and we applied imagination in order to make sense of a partial perspective. Now we encounter an overlooked volume of significance through immediate experience and, with astonishment we find a vasty richer panorama. It is as if we had been distracted by what we thought reality was and failed to actually encounter the depth of meaning beneath phenomenal appearances.

Direct cognition is unachievable unless practiced with integrity and sincerity. There is no point in trying these things halfheartedly. If we merely wish to determine what something is through our feeling nature or from an established resource of entrenched convictions then what we are doing is nothing new. But it is unfortunate if we deceive ourselves into imagining that we have attained a direct knowledge of the essential identity of something when we have not. The wonder that arises upon the direct experience of the full volume is a sufficient barometer to test the authenticity of the experience. One then begins to confidently apply direct cognition because therein resides the meaningful value of things.

Direct cognition must be practiced systematically with much the same discipline as the empirical researcher who refuses to compromise significance and value for premature results. The phenomenon is met experientially and straightforwardly without corruption through partiality or fantasy.

Materialistic, Western philosophy appears profoundly shortsighted to one who has glimpsed essential realities. It is recognized as the predictable result of a conviction whereby physical appearances receive exclusive attention. While rationale provides a structure that enables the disciplined researcher to explore tangible phenomena on the basis of their physical properties, it is inadequate when applied to those things of obvious value but which exist without material form. Intangible significances must be experienced directly in order to be known.

The capacity to explore the nature of intangible reality is a scarcely developed, human inherence. Where a trace of direct cognition is evident it is frequently accompanied by a muddle of every conceivable combination of imagination and wishful thinking. A glimpse of authentic knowledge is frequently misinterpreted through the extreme lens of materialism and mysticism and, inevitably, it loses all significance.

Conventional human understanding maintains a tenuous confidence in materialism in spite of the bleak picture of existence that it portrays. But even though materialistic, Western philosophy appears to be sustained by scientific authority, an exclusively physical interpretation of existence contradicts our own experience, and we become suspicious.

Materialistic overreach fails to encompass the intrinsic natures or things, or the intangible qualities and values that give meaning because it is an abstract, philosophical extrapolation that solely encompasses the physical extremity of existence.

The reduction of life into terms derived merely from physical properties and only comprehensible to a forced, materialistic exclusivity, is blatantly a contrived excess. Materialistic exceptionalism is a viewpoint that seems strange and obscure to those impatient with abstraction because it does not correspond with experiential reality. Furthermore, those essential qualities that are most significant to healthy, human experience are blatantly marginalized as insubstantial by an intellectual philosophy established exclusively upon physical evidence.

The intangible, essential significance of a phenomenon or of a person is impossible to describe purely in physical terms, and it is most successfully articulated through the skill of the artist. The materialist, ignoring personal experience to the contrary, insists that the substantial existence of something is exclusively physical. Consequently, the obvious appearance is exhaustively analyzed as if the essential somehow resided in the material minutiae.

For example, to the materialist, sunlight is essentially electro-magnetic radiation perhaps consisting of waves or perhaps photons. Any experientially recognizable, intangible qualities are conveniently attributed to mere physical interactions in order that they may be understood in materialistic terms. The resulting distortion of reality reduces sunlight to a phenomenon entirely lacking in value. However, the artist can express the same phenomenon in myriad terms extending from sunniness to sunbeams and through a vast palette of attributive description.

Abstract, mathematical models are painstakingly conceived that nevertheless fail to successfully describe sunlight because they endeavor to define it through numerical representation. They imagine that sunlight can be completely represented numerically while in reality the significance of daylight is qualitative, and consequently it has to be directly experienced in order to be known.

In other words, if we immediately experience sunlight we discoverer a characteristic nature that is not quantifiable. It is this event that the artist seeks to describe. That is to say, the discrepancy between abstraction and the authentic experience is only resolved through direct cognition. Sunlight is encountered for what it really is through an immediate concurrence between the observer and the phenomenon, and it is known for its actual existence to the degree that it is qualitatively apprehended. Thereby, it becomes self-evident that an abstracted definition established exclusively upon the properties of the physical appearance does not describe the actuality but merely those self-same aspects that can be quantified.

While the identity of sunlight and hence its reality cannot be fathomed solely through mathematics and physics, the contradiction for the materialist is that the quality of sunlight, while known personally and experientially, remains emphatically incommensurate when exclusively considered in physical terms. The materialist, therefore, ignores directly and experientially ascertained knowledge, and subsequently constructs an artificial interpretation that does not resemble the full reality. In the interest of empirical discipline, all information should be included in order to arrive at a definitive knowledge and not merely the easily assessed physically derived data. Intelligence concerning intangible qualities and values must be incorporated as significant in order to approach a proper explication of life.

The innate significances of a thing reveal the intrinsic nature. One recognizes the sunshine for its life enhancing quality through the direct experience of being bathed in its particular light and warmth. One could stare at the mathematics all day long and still remain ignorant of what sunlight actually is because intangible qualities have to be immediately experienced in order to be known.

For example, the difference in quality between two varieties of acorn reveals their distinctions of nature. It is the intrinsic identities and qualitative differences that need to be experienced directly in order that a thing be correctly identified. Material properties are superficial and only partially represent a phenomenon. Exclusive attention to the material condition leads to a misrepresentation of reality.

Laws are persistent, ecological influences and demands, that bear upon natural phenomena and impact their appearance. With regard to the intrinsic identity, however, physical law is non-causal. The laws of physics do not determine the inherent nature; they only effect the physical appearance. Another planet with different environmental parameters would host minerals and creatures of an appearance appropriate to that particular complex of ecological constraints. Their manner of functioning would be otherwise than upon Earth. However, the intrinsic identity of a phenomenon could be identical in both contexts.

Similarly, upon Earth the demands of natural law may vary depending on the location because of disproportionate influences. The gigantic size of the Blue Whale is only possible because the buoyant effect of saltwater compensates for the downward pull of gravity, otherwise the animal would perish of its own weight. Countless natural laws share a commonality of influence upon structure, function and appearance. However, the significance of natural law upon the intrinsic identities of creatures remains moot because it only influences the physical appearance and manner of arrangement but not the qualitative distinction.

Intrinsic identities are differentiated by their quality of expression. The one acorn variety has a shallow cupule of a fine bark-like texture. The nut lengthens to a gradual taper. Another variation has a cupule composed of soft leaf-like scales. The cupule extends three-quarters of the way towards the tip of the nut. These distinctions are the characteristic manner whereby the same oak concept is expressed alternatively. The essential nature of expression of the one tree is qualitatively different from that of another, yet they remain of the same concept. There is only one oak acorn but many variations upon the same theme.

Comparisons such as these may be further extended to explore the different qualities of expression between the acorn and, for example the walnut, in order to determine how the one differs from the other in nature and how that difference is expressed in appearance. Again, one finds there is one tree and seed principle but endless potential expression. The essential distinction between the expressions of the same concept is both a qualitative and intrinsic demonstration of a variation of character.

Similarly, different trees can be instructively compared through an examination of the qualities of the sap for its medicinal or poisonous nature: the smell of the wood; the bark; leaves; blossoms and the shape of the branches as well as the overall gesture of the tree. All these things, each within their own context, build an impression of the particular disposition of the tree.

At first, it may seem fairly easy to compare phenomena for the differences in their qualitative expression. But the quality of two tree saps are not conclusively identified through a mere subjective appraisal. In order to attain definitive identification, the observer much established a similarly intrinsic perspective.

The practice of direct, experiential cognition is only significant when the inherent identity of the human being is established as our viewpoint. The perspective of the essential, human distinction is able to determine the intrinsic existence of things through immediate engagement. This occurs because the condition of cognitive immediacy that is established between the human, unique individuality and the object of interest concerns both experiential and direct cognition. In other words, no intermediary interpretation is permitted.

Only the human, essential identity recognizes that which is intrinsic concerning the object. Consequently, there is nothing separating the immediate cognition of the human, unique individuality and the object of observation. The singular, human distinction engages the phenomenon and encounters the authentic condition of the existence of the thing through immediate experience. Thus, direct cognition may be described as a wordless, experiential encounter between the self and the particular object of interest.

While the definitive existence of the phenomenal world was held in suspicion through the abstract reasoning of the seventeenth-century philosopher René Descartes, in reality, existence is not misrepresented by the physical senses when once the human, essential singularity directly engages a situation. Had Descartes directly experienced phenomena through an immediate encounter through the aegis of his *I am,* he would have discovered not only the intrinsic particularity of things but also that the distinction between phenomena exists as an intangible dimension that qualifies physical conditions with meaning.

Cerebral thinking works indirectly with ideas and concepts. It tries to work out and identify a phenomenon based upon the match of new data to existing preconceptions. It endeavors to do so imaginatively and speculatively in order to approximate one thing with another. This is a practice far removed from cognition through immediate engagement. A direct encounter of the phenomenal world does not require the estimation of what something may be, but apprehends the intrinsic nature of phenomenal existence through the experiential straightforwardness of the individual ipseity.

The phenomenal world can be physically scrutinized for its properties and imaginatively construed through a sequence of logical postulation, but by such means, phenomena will always only remain superficially assessed. However, immediate experiential engagement and the concomitant knowledge concerning the intrinsic nature of the existence of things, reveal the essential volume of things through the aegis of the human individual self.

In order that the human mind may directly encounter and engage the essential significance of a thing, the busy intellect and affected partiality must be temporarily restrained. This is because intangible significances have to be directly experienced in order to be recognized, and nothing can be allowed to inhibit straightforward engagement. In other words, neither reason nor sentiment is required for the practice of immediate cognition.

We are used to considering phenomena indirectly and abstractly but immediate cognition deals only with the experientially discernible, intangible dimension of existence that cannot be adequately recognized solely through our conventional cognitive practices. That which is experienced directly by the human, essential individuality is authenticated as real because the self as the authentic identity of the human being is the ultimate, qualitative benchmark of absolute reality.

2. DIRECT, EXPERIENTIAL COGNITION
Uninhibited, Cognitive Encounter through the Mind-Self

It is disturbing that anyone whether they be priest, scholar or scientist should assume a monopoly of interpretation and emphatically inform the layman as to what life is all about. Furthermore, it is perplexing that there are so many contradictory yet apparently unequivocal interpretations of existence. Even within the same disciplines there exists only tenuous consensus, and each jurisdiction describes life in terms of their own particular specialty. However, based upon so many obvious contradictions one can only conclude that comprehensive authority is unattainable and that we cannot posses the definitive knowledge that we claim. It remains, therefore, the responsibility of the individual to explore and discover reality for oneself.

Direct cognition is an uninhibited activity of understanding whereby the conventual interpretative faculties are intentionally restrained to allow unmediated sentience. It is an original and entirely straightforward approach that concerns immediate engagement instead of the familiar oblique practice of perception. Thereby, something becomes known without describing, classifying or reducing the experience into different terms. Consequently, an object is discovered not as it is superficially represented or interpreted, but for its intrinsic significance.

In other words, through immediate cognition, the mind straightforwardly experiences the identity of the object of interest and knows it at once for its existential significance. The phenomenon is apprehended without any kind of cerebral or sentimental representation, and it is met directly and experienced for what it is without arbitrary appraisal.

An immediate, non-cerebral and unaffected cognitive activity as described here, is a contrary approach to our normal human practice of thinking and feeling evaluation. Conventionally, the acquisition of knowledge is imagined to be ideally objective and decisive through the abstract consideration of the quantifiable data that can be calculated. But qualitative information cannot be justified in the same way as the physical, and its significance is consequently treated with suspicion and disparaged as merely subjectively determined.

Immediate, experiential cognition does not attempt to evaluate and assess a phenomenon through calculation or logical process. It is an activity of discernment that occurs directly between the mind and an object of interest whereby the phenomenon is directly encountered without partiality. That is to say, the opposite of objectivity does not have to be ambiguousness, but through discipline, physically elusive conditions can be objectively observed with as much transparency as material circumstances.

The unique, respective mind is the authentic identity of a person. Unlike the superficial appearance, the individual, essential significance possesses intrinsic being, and it recognizes itself only through the profundity of immediate, experiential cognition.

The singular mind may discover itself by direct engagement, but it can also discern the crucial significance of all other phenomena. In other words, the essential human being discovers the authentic condition of the existence of things because, as an entity, it is able to directly experience similarly substantive conditions.

Furthermore, through the recognition of the individual authenticity of another person from the perspective of one's own intrinsic distinction, we experience non-sentimental love. The superficial properties are overlooked and thereupon the substantial identity becomes evident. Thus, the other is not assessed and evaluated upon the merits of their appearance nor upon the basis of our preferences but recognized for their essential and unique significance.

Popular misrepresentation insists that the mind, the body and the self are somehow synonymous. Indeed, the brain is granted precedence and unique status as the seat of human identity while all the other organs and arrangements receive merely functional distinction. Our circulatory system or digestive structure appears to have no identity at all while the neural organization is said to embody the human particularity, in much the same way as the heart was formerly recognized and continued, as the linguistic epitome of love.

Be that as it may, the human, unique individuality discovers its distinctive existence by direct experiential cognition through the assertion of its authority as the essential significance of the human constitution. Thereupon, we directly observe and recognize our uniqueness but fail to attribute the same to any organ or biological function. Indeed, the substantive human entity is inherently distinguished from the corporeal vehicle, and we no longer confuse the organism with the intrinsic host.

Fine art is the ideal language whereby qualitative, intangible significances may be described. While essential conditions may be directly engaged by the particular, human entity, they cannot be quantified in the manner of the physical but they must be represented through artistic analogy.

The following sculptural representation, *Day,* by Michelangelo Buonarroti (1475-1564), reveals something of the quality of the awakening human authority, the essential entity. There is no intermediation apparent in the direct and straightforward gaze. It comes from deep beyond, penetrating into the depths of things seeking the essential and meaningful. The powerful musculature epitomizes the direct and forthright nature of immediate cognition.

The essential entity, distinguished from the human, physical architecture through the aegis of immediate, experiential cognition, is alone capable of discerning the essential caliber of phenomena. It discerns the authentic identity of another and also the inherent constitution of all phenomena. Immediate access to intrinsic knowledge through direct experience is a significant but neglected fundament of the human constitution. However, unless it is experienced for oneself, knowledge concerning the substantive nature of things will be readily confused with sentimental evaluation or heightened spontaneous association and summarily dismissed.

But immediate cognition is not so easily refuted because it concerns the inherent, cognitive capacity resident within the essential constitution of every human being. To deny straightforward engagement is to reject the significance of the human entity. If we consider ourselves merely biological then further qualitative development is effectively precluded.

Conventionally, a phenomenon is evaluated through an aggregation of various degrees of sentimentally and reasoning. However, scientifically, we approach phenomena through a discipline that forestalls subjective evaluation. The mental activity of the observer or researcher endeavors to reasonably reconcile established preconceptions and associations with new information. We reason and deduce, trying to establish a construct and an understanding based upon previous concepts.

Similarly, immediate cognition requires the methodical and impartial approach of empiricism. We have no interest whatsoever in pretense. Indeed, the discovery of the essential significance of phenomena is prevented by predilections, and the entire exercise is rendered moot.

Direct cognition by the human, essential distinction is achieved when the habitual practice of evaluation is postponed in order that the object of interest may be recognized without the interference of preconceptions, logical inference or sentimental attachment. When the mind steadily confronts a scenario without attempting to explain or evaluate it, it gains direct access and knowledge of the reality of the existence of the phenomenon itself.

The ipseity of the human being has the capacity to discern the qualitative and inherent value of phenomena. Elemental significance is directly experienced by the human intrinsic selfhood because the essential person is an entity that exists in the same elemental condition as the intrinsic existence of phenomena. Essential knowledge, directly recognized, is qualitatively different from conventional intelligence. The latter is an indirect approach while immediate cognition is an impendent encounter.

Direct, experiential cognition is not the activity of sensing or of instinct. While animals very poorly deduce and reason, nevertheless they sense, detect and discover with acuteness through an impressive feeling nature. Creatures examine and sift and sense in order to ascertain and evaluate their activities according to their particular natures. They do so through native ability and heightened, collective sensitivity beyond the conventional organs of detection.

Humans experience these sensations but in animals they are heightened through an exclusively speechless organization. Even animal sounds and calls are direct expressions of a feeling-sentient constitution. These moods, passions and instincts become the animal's seat of cognition. In other words, animals feel their way through life.

A similar sensing capacity is recognizable as a fickle and inconstant sort of sixth sense in human beings that, when further enhanced, initially seems impressive and oracular. But such practices do not resemble the caliber of knowledge attained through immediate experience because they do not pertain to essential existence. In other words, elementary understanding through immediate engagement has nothing at all to do with the human feeling nature.

The activity of immediate cognition and the experience of concomitant, direct knowledge is a thoroughly conscious one. The seat of individual human identity is removed from a bodily misidentification to its rightful precedent as the incorporeal, individual mind. The essential, human distinction is always conscious but for the most part we remain unaware of it and assume a lesser corporeal and superficial identity.

Human volition must redirect attention and establish the prerogative of the entity as the essential, individual significance and the seat of authority within the human constitution. The respective distinction, as the unique individuality of the human being, is the paramount authority and enduring reality of the human constitution. This is discovered experientially through immediate cognition, but it cannot be known through rationale.

3. PHYSICAL APPEARANCES
The Restricted Mentality of the Materialist

A pre-established, dogmatic conviction will always inhibit the exploration of a perspective that inadvertently challenges it. While everyone experiences and engages qualitative value during daily life, denying intangibly extant information at their peril, conversely, the materialistic construct is established solely open the evidence of tangible, material properties. It is this selectivity that make materialistic exclusivity a contrived philosophy.

The contradiction between individual first-hand knowledge and a theory established upon pretentious, misconceived conjecture, indicates how an abstract interpretation of life can become accepted, and can significantly narrow and constrain our understanding within parameters that do not realistically exist. Thereby, exaggerated systems and theories are established upon professional sanction, and subsequently we struggle to explain life in exclusively within artificial terms.

The practice of cognition through immediate experience is not another theory. It is a straightforward approach towards understanding the essential significance of physical phenomena. Yet, presently we encounter resistance because the materialist necessarily thinks in the abstract terms of the philosophy of physicalism. Consequently, while immediate cognition requires the direct application of the human, essential existence, the materialist categorically denies the existence of an incorporeal, human essence even though myriad, other intangible significances are our constant experience. Thus, materialistic, Western philosophy obstructs original inquiry through a predetermined dogmatism that hinders open-minded exploration.

Nevertheless, concerning a receptive readership, the concept of direct cognition through the aegis of the unique, individual distinction of the human being may be readily grasped as an intellectual concept but it is of no significant value unless it is applied. Consequently, the essential prerequisite of the direct approach, is not understanding, as such, but the experiential recognition of the authentic identity of the human being. It makes no sense at all to suggest that immediate, pragmatic engagement is possible through conventional rationale. If that were so, we might have understood and would have adopted the practice of immediate discernment long ago. In any event, direct cognition has nothing to do with the intellect or the human, feeling nature, but it concerns the intrinsic human entity.

This is an enormously difficult concept for the reasoning mind to grasp and indeed it cannot do so unless we experientially recognize the essential significance of the human being. It is from the perspective of our intrinsic existence that immediate, experiential cognition is possible and not through conventional understanding. Experiential cognition requires direct involvement while indirect deduction and feeling assessment remain our familiar and trusted approaches but are nevertheless insufficient. Consequently, information concerning the essential distinction of phenomena, through the direct engagement of the mind without reliance upon the intellect, remains inconceivable from the perspective of standard reasoning.

In other terms, the establishment of an intellective model of any form, will inevitably obscure original knowledge derived through immediate experience. Consequently, a philosophical conviction that emphatically denies the significance of non-physical existence inevitably hinders the exploration of immediate cognition because direct engagement is only established through the intrinsic, human existence and not by a corporeal function.

Probably the most significant entomologist the world has ever known, Jean-Henri Fabre (1823 – 1915), and the equally prestigious Scottish biologist and mathematician, D'Arcy Wentworth Thompson (1850 – 1948), remain recognized and respected for their astute observation. They both resisted minimizing and understating the objects of their investigation and avoided the establishment of theoretical structures, theories and systems in order to explain them. They were consequently, sufficiently open-minded and receptive to explore anything unconventional that their researches might unexpectedly tender. For this reason, all possibilities remained negotiable to their unbiased approach, and their researches were entirely original.

The open, untrammeled mind is able to apprehend a phenomenon on terms intrinsic to the object of interest itself. The receptive, unprejudiced and open-minded perspective considers inconvenient contradictions to established views with interest and explores their implications, knowing full well that nothing in reality is as simple or circumscribed as the human intellect would prefer it to be.

It is unproductive to attempt to address the

inadequacy of materialistic, Western philosophy with the sectarian dogmatist who is convinced of its justification. The pedant defends a hypothetical assumption as if it were a religion but new insights require a willingness on our part to concede to the possibility of a different approach than merely the entrenched consensus. As we have already discussed, the direct cognitive approach entails the recognition and subsequent application of the incorporeal essential of the human constitution and of phenomena, the existence of which the materialist will flatly deny because qualitative differentiation is a proportion of the material appearance that is not physically apparent.

While the incorporeal identity of the human being cannot be physically identified, it can be discovered experientially. It is here that the dogmatic materialist once more objects to an active exploration of direct cognition because it is assumed that knowledge through immediate experience is inevitably subjective. However, uninhibited sentience is similarly restrained along with the intellect in order that the direct encounter between the respective mind and a phenomenon remain entirely original.

The mentality that recognizes as valid, only the physical appearance of a phenomenon cannot comprehend an activity of perception that suggests that the human, individual entity is capable of the direct apprehension of essential significances. Neither the concept of human ipseity, nor the elemental consequence of phenomena, can supersede the certain conviction of biological and material exclusivity. Nevertheless, the essential individual can immediately engage circumstances both because the individual exists as an emphatic entity, and through the implicitness of a more profound volume of meaning than the blatant appearance of things.

The materialist maintains that something cannot exist unless it is physically represented. The only reliable cognitive activity that is recognized is cerebral and, therefore, the incorporeal mind and the physical brain are conveniently considered as synonymous terms for the biological organ.

The intellectual position which insists that only physical matter has reality, relies upon a process of logical calculation and assessment carefully established upon exclusively material evidence, in order to determine what a phenomenon is. It is horrified at the mere suggestion of a direct, cognitive approach through an elusive, human component and attributes the proposal to misguided belief or fiction. It would indeed remain a mere belief if it were not substantiated through immediate experience. The practice of cognition through direct encounter cannot be adequately reasoned but must be directly justified. It requires the experiential recognition of the human, authentic identity whose existence the materialist emphatically denies on the grounds of intangibility. But through immediate cognition we find that human uniqueness is not the same as the brain but it is the essential identity of the human being and it is this individual entity that is able to exercise direct cognition.

The materialist further claims that directly ascertained knowledge is the result of a random rearrangement of preconceptions and associations that automatically and capriciously amalgamate to present an appropriate solution. This explanation suggests of a similar random occurrence attributed to cellular and genetic coordination. The materialist seems to enjoy the convenient expediency of spontaneous organization even though in human affairs we battle constantly against entropy and thereby demonstrate that practical arrangement is far from spontaneous.

Materialistic, Western philosophy cannot conceive of anything but measurably, tangible properties, therefore, every phenomenon without a visible provocation as its origin is allocated a random and capricious inception without predictable cause.

However, the activity of direct cognition through the immediate experience of the mind-self is not capricious but the result of specific and concerted attention by the singular individual. When unhindered by the cerebral, material counterpart or by feeling-sentience, it can engage a phenomenon free from the paraphrasing of indirect, abstract or intermediary interpretation. Thereupon, the essential individual directly engages and experiences a phenomenon for what that thing intrinsically is.

An exploration of the dynamic of immediate cognition will not persuade the staunch materialist who is already convinced of an exclusively tangible existence. That mentality will have to manage on a lean and frugal perspective restricted to the physical because it can neither conceive nor respect the existence of anything of significance beyond that revealed by a scrutiny of material condition. It considers knowledge concerning intangible realities to be merely, muddled imagination because materially unfounded, it deems them unrealistic irrespective of the fact that we must withhold feeling-sentience, association and rationale in order to engage circumstances originally and pristinely.

The reasoned approach cannot attempt to challenge materialism upon its own terms because immediate cognition only uses material phenomena as a focal point or center of attention. That is, the appearance is the shallow view that serves to anchor our observation of the essential nature. Consequently, materialism will always remain antagonistic and obstructive by virtue of its physical partiality. But once an interested individual stays conventional, materialistic prejudice and experientially discovers their own authentic condition of existence, the legitimate nature of things appears self-evidently quite different from the accepted condition.

The exclusive, physical perspective is myopic, restricted to the indirectly, envisaged concepts of the intellect that deny reality to anything incorporeal. The materialist will always despise the concept of intangible existence as a notion akin to delusion because, from a strictly materialistic perspective, existence cannot be independent of a physical phenomenon.

But immediately determined knowledge involves a direct encounter by the human, unique identity. Meanwhile, the brain remains a physical property of the material constitution of the human being, that inevitably functions obliquely and abstractly. But the brain is not an entity, and consequently it cannot know anything through immediate encounter because it cannot directly experience but must always evaluate things remotely.

The human, essential mind does not have physical substance and therefore, it is able, through immediate cognition to recognize the substantive, incorporeal significance of other phenomena. Since the particular entity recognizes a similar elementary imperative as its own, in other phenomena, it does not have to figure something out indirectly but it knows of its nature instantaneously. Similarly, the existence of the mind-self is only recognized through direct cognition because it is intangible and purely essential in nature and must be experienced directly in order to be known. In other words, self-recognition is achieved only through direct experience.

  The intrinsic, qualitative value and the inherent nature of all phenomena is essentially intangible. In ordinary day-to-day existence intangibles are not overlooked but they are known experientially. In real life, qualitative values cannot be denied, yet philosophies and theories that define existence in exclusively material terms abound and present a fabricated and abstract perspective towards existence that is void of profound meaning. However, phenomena without intangible value represent a mere carapace of our everyday experience and the discrepancy between such a philosophy and our own knowledge rightfully leaves us perplexed. Furthermore, it is extraordinary how the shallow counterfeit continues to insinuate itself and confounds wholesome understanding.

  For example, the difference between a tomato freshly picked from the garden, where it was grown in rich healthy soil and sun-ripened, compared with the factory farmed produce that is picked green for convenient shipping and gassed with chemicals in order to achieve a red hue, is apparent to the gardener and consumer alike. Yet, when analyzed both tomatoes are found to consist of essentially, identical substances. The properties that can be calibrated and accounted through analysis are solely physical but the qualitative value that differentiate the garden tomato from the factory alternative is extraordinarily significant. However, while we know that the two differ enormously in taste, smell and goodness, commercial interests continue to claim that the appearance supersedes the inherent value. Even though the one is a healthy and enjoyable meal eaten raw while the other is barely palatable and must be cooked and seasoned, nevertheless the materialistic view predominates.

Fortunately, more and more, the consumer justifiably refuses to accept the results of physical analysis as definitive proof concerning quality because our own experience is entirely at odds with those results. The analysis is biased, merely accounting for the physical properties, while, in reality, everything has significant qualitative, intangible value that cannot be overlooked if we wish to understand existence as it really is.

It is hard to describe the experience of the quality of a sun-ripened tomato, a breathtaking landscape or a friendship, but to deny them reality is patently absurd. But this is what materialistic philosophies attempt. The physical and easily assimilated properties are extracted from the phenomenon while the intangible, qualitative dimension of existence is interpreted in materialistic terms as if all values are successfully quantifiable.

Qualitative value cannot be adequately evaluated nor understood through quantification because intangible significances are only comprehensively recognized experientially, but not numerically or by physical analysis.

Thus, the qualitative value of a color is reduced to a wavelength, and the materialist insists that numerical calibration is all that the color really is. The intangible reality that is experientially and directly known conflicts the materialistic supposition and it is conveniently disregarded.

In a similar way that art is the ideal language of experientially discovered, qualitative value, the essential cannot be reasoned unless it is reduced to its few quantifiable properties whereby the intangible content will be entirely lost in the process. To the degree that the artist is capable of an immediate experience of the intangible, qualitative value of something and, depending on the skill level of the individual in the particular artistic medium, incorporeal realities can be successfully communicated.

However, the emphasis upon reduced, quantifiable properties and the attempt to define all of life's experiences in those terms has reached levels whereby the materialistic mentality has gained overwhelming predominance at the expense of the physically elusive but meaningful value of phenomena. Consequently, a pernicious, mechanistic world-view is prevalent whereby the essential, incorporeal identity of the human being is negated or considered imaginary, along with the qualitative content and intangible value inherent to all other phenomena.

The analytical, physical approach that declares both the garden and the factory tomatoes to be identical is applied indiscriminately and sweepingly, establishing a materialistic philosophy and world-view that has hoodwinked humanity into believing that life is void of significant meaning. In effect, life portrayed without qualitative value is a fraudulent misrepresentation. In reality the human being does not exist within those terms and a philosophy or theoretical construct that presents an exclusively, materialistic approach as reality impoverishes human understanding and subsequent experience.

Qualitative values are essentially intangible in nature, and consequently they can only be realistically known through immediate experience. Yet, they remain as real and as important as the quantifiable, material properties and their recognition is of enormous significance to human wellbeing. A structure or philosophical system that defines life excluding qualitative and essential merit is recognized merely as an artificial contrivance and deserves to be treated with incredulity.

Immediate experience alone reveals the inherent value of a phenomenon but it is through the aegis of the mind-self that we are able to discern the intangible dimension of the existence of something by the discipline of objectivity. This is achievable because the essential individual engages things directly without interpretation. Through direct cognition, the human, unique entity meets the reality of the qualitative dimension straightforwardly and discovers both its authenticity and existential significance.

4. INCORPOREAL REALITY
The Folly of the Materialistic Denial of the Intangible

There is a blatant discrepancy between an exclusively materialistic position towards existence and the subsequent definition of life solely in physical terms, and life as it is experienced in reality even by the most determined materialist. The dogma founded merely upon knowledge of the material aspects of phenomena does not correspond with our everyday reality. The exclusively, materialistic theory is an inadequate definition of life because it excludes experiential reality. If life were really lived solely upon materialistic terms, it would be unbelievably depressing because it would be void of meaning and value. While the abstract thinker enjoys the tidiness of a comprehensive formula that appears to explain phenomena on a predictable and tangible footing and endorses it as a creed, nevertheless it must comprise the entirety or it is irrelevant. But the dogma of the materialist through its selective bias lacks perspicacity. It is a superficial and unsound interpretation that inadequately describes practical life. Composed merely of the tangible and measurable attributes, it inevitably offers an unreal world-view exclusively established upon the most obvious properties.

In practice an abstract, materialistic formula requires that everything be reduced to its own symbolic logic, tangible obviousness and stark simplicity. Thus, the most blatant mechanical and lifeless features of matter are applied as the foundation of a world-view. Consequently, both the human Mind and the conscious individuality is conveniently equated with the brain which is the only conceivable, physical component of the body that is suitable. The consequences of this conceptual legerdemain are untenable because realistically even the most ardent materialist cannot seriously identify unique distinction with a physical organ because otherwise every organ of the human body must also assume a similar autonomy. Just as one can hardly claim that the physical heart really loves, no more can the brain be exaggerated to assume the incorporeal significance of human individual identity.

However, a closed mind, having accepted an abstract construct of someone else's conception, claims that the unproven hypothesis, when sufficiently elaborated, is beyond challenge merely on the strength of the consensus of the supporters. Thus, predispositional enchantment prevents the examination of anything that may contradict those basic materialistic tenets. If a challenge is mounted, the established convictions are so fragile that the materialist must defensively ridicule any other perspective. Such is the intensity of philosophical fidelity that by this expedient, the contentious and theoretical nature of a perspective does not have to be rethought or reevaluated, and indeed there is usually little interest or palette to do so.

The materialist who rebuffs even the possibility of another and more profound activity of cognition because of a personal satisfaction with an established conception, is forced to remain within the confines and limits of a circumscribed position. The irony is that the adopted concepts are frequently unoriginal and merely observed through allegiance, but not by practical inquiry and cognizance. That is to say, an accepted authority establishes a determinedly argued hypothesis that becomes accepted as valid without proof. Nevertheless, unproven, it remains merely a belief alike to any other.

The essential identity of the individual human being is an incorporeal reality. It does not have a physical basis nor is it materially identifiable. In order to be known, it has to be directly experienced. It cannot be demonstrated abstractly nor can its authenticity be satisfactorily argued. It is not the same as the brain. The brain can indeed be identified through physical examination. The human, unique individuality is of an entirely different distinction.

The materialist will work tirelessly to discover new qualifications that reinforce the notion that the body and, in particular, the brain is the only identifiable human identity. From the perspective of abstract thinking this appears sound reasoning because indirect evaluation cannot comprehend realities which must be experienced in order to be known. But the authentic, human individuality has the capacity to directly apprehend a phenomenon. Consequently, when the mind-self engages an object directly it is able to discern the essential and intangible condition of existence and not merely the superficial and obvious appearance. In other words, the mind-self encounters an object immediately and discovers the inherent, particular significance that is not physically conspicuous.

If an individual is willing to concede to the possibility that the identity of the human being that uses the word "I" to describe itself, does indeed enjoy essential status then it is not a long journey from there to the application of immediate cognition and the realization that direct experience reveals a far more profound quality of existence than can be ascertained through the blatant appearance. But it is essential that the self be directly and experientially known in order that other phenomena can be apprehended authentically. In other words, the human essential identity must be established as the benchmark and paramount cognitive perspective whereby things may be directly and originally encountered.

Immediately experienced, essential significances cannot be ascertained cerebrally. Holding the calculating, reasoning activity of the intellect at bay, the unique mind-self experiences and recognizes its own identity. The self then confronts other phenomena in the same direct manner. It knows authenticity because it discovers itself as ultimately authentic. The essential nature of all other things can then be readily recognize through the same cognitive practice of an immediate encounter with which the mind-self first discovered its own reality.

How strange it is that we choose to deny experiential validation of the existence of our own selves in order to maintain an abstractly conceived structure. This occurs because the intellect, with its capacity to reason logically towards a conclusion appears to be the only reliable, cognitive authority. But reason cannot discover nor comprehend incorporeal reality and, consequently, the autonomous self, that is so essential to direct cognition, is denied validity. Without the authority of the conscious self, conclusive knowledge concerning something that cannot be calculated is impossible.

The denial of the existence of the essential self reveals a prejudice for indirect conceptualization over immediate experience. The intellectual would rather figure something out than empirically engage a phenomenon because the authority of logic appears to offer greater reliability than the testimony of direct cognition.

The proposal that the human, essential identity is incorporeal and can be directly known as such seems a slight matter compared to the materialistic theory that asserts that order and organization spontaneously and capriciously arose through impartial physical forces. One wonders how physical forces void of imagination might prove to be so incredibly resourceful and inventive.

If a person could for one moment experiences the reality of the incorporeal, in juxtaposition to conceptual abstraction and grasp that immediate cognition avoids the need for conventional rationalization, then a disciplined inquiry would be enthusiastically forthcoming. The stubborn materialist merely obstructs others in this pursuit with emphatic and dogmatic statements as if reasoning alone can achieve definitive knowledge. In practice, reason manipulates concepts most inefficiently, and it is consistently demonstrated as ambiguous through the evidence of its conclusions. Consequently, it is valid to describe the reasoning capacity of the human being as most ideally suited to systematic and sequential deduction. Mathematics are the perfect example of that ideal. But the more remote deductive reasoning is from the ideal circumstances of computation the less precisely it operates.

The mentality that can only comprehend material evidence cannot explore immediate cognition because the incorporeal significance of the human being is its requisite agency. Yet, while the intellect remains mystified in terms of incorporeal reality, it cannot, in fact, forestall or avoid it. In practice, intangible realities constantly confront human experience, but the artificial, intellectual construct of the materialist excludes that knowledge from the equation, insisting upon a stark, exclusively physical interpretation of life that is remote from actual reality.

The belief that any human being can think solely through the intellectual assessment of material conditions is a fallacy. The physical properties of phenomena that serve as the foundation for abstract, materialistic theories and definitions of life, when considered alone, present a morbid distortion. No one lives their lives void of intangible, qualitative values. When those values are removed through an abstract assessment of life or reduced to mechanical and physical fundamentals, a nonsense replaces reality. The argument of the materialist is that everything must be tangible in order to be deemed authentic. Yet, no one can be a pure materialist because it is untenable contrivance. Real life does not consist exclusively of material properties. To deny intangible values is to reduce life to an artificial, mechanical construct. Yet, this is the sustained conceit of materialistic, abstract reasoning even though it is demonstrated as unreasonable in practice.

It is this discrepancy between what the materialist espouses and the practical inability of the human being to perform exclusively under those terms that needs attention. Under the facade of science, whereby every investigator pretends an aura of authority while presenting abstract theories irrespective of a lack of empirical discipline, the physical is elevated to a position of exclusive significance. Thereby, intangible values and qualitative realities that cannot be intellectually represented are discounted from the theory while, nevertheless, they cannot be avoided in practice because they are both real and conspicuous enough to enrich or impoverish our lives. Abstract theories and systems, however erudite, pale miserably when compared to directly, experienced reality.

When a postulate remains empirically unproven, it cannot be considered reliable. It remains at the stage of a hypothesis. But modern philosophy allows a theory to stand if it is considered well argued and supported by sufficient consensus. Thus, it is accepted as conclusive through peer concurrence and a mockery is made of the empirical process. It would be fair to say that much that is accepted as fact is no more than informed conjecture. The materialist requires that intangible values be considered suspect, yet fails to append the same caveat to abstractly reasoned, un-demonstrated, materialistically established theories. The exclusive monopoly claimed by the materialist to define life solely in physical terms is an imposition that leads to a gross misinterpretation of life.

When the materialist is presented with a question, the answer consistently arises from the perspective of an established philosophical conviction. It is always abstract because it is always only an indirect evaluation. Compared to original experience an entrenched position merely molds a response according to the parameters and restraints of a pre-established conviction.

However, we are exploring direct cognition because we find that deductions founded upon worked-over associations provide only very unsatisfactory knowledge of existence and we wish to discover things in their original condition where they exist definitively.

It is of no interest what we *think* something is. We wish to know what it is in reality, in its own right without interference from our own particular preconceptions, associations and sentiments. If one desires definitive knowledge it cannot be deduced from opinions, memories and the indirect workings of the intellect. Consequently, if we desire to know something for certain then, the phenomenon has to be addressed directly and experientially without interference from rationale. If one wishes to know the essential identity of a thing then one must search for its inherent existence. The appearance alone will not suffice.

In other words, one cannot indirectly reason the intrinsic nature of a phenomenon because it exists essentially, and consequently it can only be experientially identified. A theory that presumes that life consists only of those properties that can be physically justified must deny everything else that cannot be assessed in the same way. That premise inevitably excludes qualities and values and paints a stark, morbid and counterfeit assessment of existence that contradicts our own experience.

5. THE HUMAN MIND-SELF
Recognition of Essential Identity of the Human Being

The value of immediate engagement as a definitive, cognitive approach is only appreciable through experience. The conventional, intellectual and emotional practices of understanding will attempt to evaluate the practice of direct cognition upon the strength of familiar but indirect terms of assessment. Direct cognition is thereby trivialized because it cannot be understood in the manner of a concept but it must be immediately investigated in order to be befittingly adjudicated.

The manner whereby phenomena may be directly engaged and the inherent distinction of their existence discerned, is through the immediate employment of the human singularity. The human, unique ipseity that essentially distinguishes each one of us, is the mind-self. If we seek to physically identify our intrinsic individuality, we will be unable to do from a physical point-of-view because the body will appear to represent all the characteristic differences. But in reality, individual significance exists intangibly and may only be discovered through the immediate, cognitional encounter of the essential self.

The first step is to undeniably demonstrate the existence of intangible reality and draw attention to the failings of a theoretical construct that dismisses qualitative realities because they are not physically represented. Contrary to popular, materialistic philosophy, in myriad ways during the events of ordinary life every human being is intimately involved with intangible significances. The discrepancy between a contrived construct and direct experience should reveal the shortcomings of an exclusively materialistic point of view that is in reality untenable. The perspective that acknowledges the exclusivity of the material while denying the validity of the experientially known intangible value of things does not work in practice.

The qualitative realities that the materialist cannot in practice deny are negated by indirectly attributing them to a material source. Thus, aspiration, inspiration and insight are all attributed to biochemical and neural causes. The color variations of daylight, the reality of life itself and the extraordinary phenomenon of human self-consciousness are all materially explained and minimized as various, mechanical functions.

However, this is only a paradoxical situation for the one who wishes to explain to an entrenched mind, an unconventional perspective. The materialist is already convinced of the relevancy of physical scrutiny in the pursuit of understanding. Indeed, there is considerable justification supporting the material approach if we merely wish to apprehend the physics of things. Accordingly, the conventional practice deals with the way a thing functions while immediate experience and knowledge through direct cognition reveals what something intrinsically is. In other words, the immediate, cognitive encounter discerns the inherent identity of a thing.

Unfortunately, the consequences of physical analysis have become applied to establish a narrow philosophy of existence within material parameters, and thereby they have indiscriminately encroached upon areas wherein calculation cannot decisively function. Deliberation and rationale may be able to determine how and why a thing works but they do not possess the capacity to conclusively identify the intrinsic condition of the existence of a phenomenon. However, it is upon the strength of misapplication that we understand why the materialistic approach to existence makes only very limited sense.

The difficulty is that the capacity to know the inherent reality of a phenomenon resides not as the faculty or function of a physical organ but within the incorporeal, human identity itself. That is too much for the confirmed materialist to contemplate. Even supposing, in principle, that immediate experience is recognized as having cognitive value, physicalism will inevitably attribute experientially derived information as if it were an extension of physical activity.

Furthermore, experiential knowledge concerning the nature of the existence of a thing is imagined to be merely subjective. But subjectivity is hardly very far removed from acceptable scientific practice when it comes to advanced physics. Upon an oblique premise, the philosophical extension of a situation, and subsequent conclusions that can never be empirically or definitively justified, appear with frequency. In other words, an unverifiable theory is adopted by consensus because it is abstractly convincing. Unfortunately, upon the concurrence of a scientific majority informed speculation may garner validation while resting merely upon argument and conjecture, and not absolute knowledge.

Without the personal experience of experientially derived knowledge through immediate cognition, no one has the authority to evaluate its significance. However, the predictable response of the materialist is to assume that direct engagement is no more than subjective assessment. Consequently, immediate cognition is reduced to an idiosyncratic practice by the rationale of those who know nothing about it, and it is summarily dismissed.

The unusual nature of the practice of directly experiencing inherent identities and qualities, is compounded when it is realized that one is engaging phenomena non-verbally and without preconception. The encounter is an original and direct occurrence between the essential human being and the phenomenon. The intrinsic condition that belies the physical appearance is thereby, immediately recognized.

This is the considerable source of protest by the materialist. An entrenched view that is established solely upon physical evidence, cannot countenance the proposition of metaphysical reality. It is the suggestion of extra-physical significance that irritates the physicalist because the prospect of physically elusive conditions threatens the foundation of what amounts to a very restricted worldview.

When an investigator restrains the usual cerebral practices and the relentless, conceptual busyness and association, so that observation may remain untainted by interpretation and by the comparison of new events with past concepts, an unconventional manner of cognition becomes possible. Sentimental distraction and cerebral activity are quieted, and an immediate interaction between the mind-self and the object of observation subsequently occurs. The authentic identity of the human observer is allowed direct and unhindered access to the phenomenon through the restraint of usual apprehension, and the essential reality of the situation becomes evident.

The authentic identity of the human being is of incorporeal, existential significance, and it is here identified as the mind-self. The mind-self can attain the unique position of immediate cognition when unhindered by intellectual and emotional preconceptions. The mind-self directly confronts the object of inquiry and recognizes it for its authentic condition of existence because the mind-self is intrinsically extant and similarly recognized only through direct experience.

The mind-self finds a qualitative counterpart in the essential of the object of the encounter. That is to say, the intrinsic identity of the human being has the capacity to engage and experience a phenomenon in terms of its essential significance, and identify its permanence. The permanence that belies the material transience is the actual condition of the existence of a thing. Thereby, immediate experience requires no interpretation but knows the authenticity of the object in an original and first-hand manner. The mind-self, confronting the phenomenon without any intermediary, discerns and recognizes the epitome of the existence of a thing because it is itself elementary.

Typically, we consider objects and events through the indirect practice of matching a phenomenon to our already established opinions and interpretations. Furthermore, we understand the workings of something through reason and ingenuity. But if we only consider things abstractly and circuitously in that fashion, there is an immediate discordance between an understanding of the exclusive, physical condition of an object and the more profound, intrinsic significance.

However, the mind-self is able to experience phenomena as if for the very first time, entirely avoiding the usual indirect representation through preconceptions or sentiment. Thus, the object is seen in an essential, untainted way and recognized for what it is. Through immediacy, it is experienced essentially, as opposed to peripherally as an abstract preconception or by evaluation through reasoning.

The existence of mind-self cannot be determined through the usual manner of cerebral thinking. It cannot be measured or calibrated as it has no distinct corporeal attributes. To cede authenticity to an incorporeal value is entirely contrary to conventional understanding whereby some tangible aspect must be sought in order that something can be satisfactorily validated. If something obviously only exists as a value, the usual practice involves an attempt to reduce it somehow into factors that can be quantifiably managed.

Furthermore, one cannot become aware of the mind-self through reduction and analysis, nor can it be identified in the same way that one determines the nature of a tangible object. It is an incorporeal entity that is, nevertheless, recognized as authentic by immediate experience.

The incorporeal value of phenomena, their intrinsic distinction and qualitative nature, defy measurement and calibration because they exist immediately, on an entirely different basis than the physical.

In summary, the myriad and impressive accomplishments through a vast range of scientific and technical research insinuate a certain exclusivity of knowledge attainable solely through the methodical scrutiny of tangible factors. This materialistic penchant has developed into a philosophical monopoly so that essential and inherently, formless values that remain beyond the reach of an otherwise exclusively tangible research, are considered of questionable reality.

Values that cannot be determined through conventional physical means can, nevertheless, be recognized through the inherent capacity of the mind-self to confront a phenomenon directly. Similarly, the mind-self, as an incorporeal entity, can validate itself and realize its own authenticity through the same activity of immediate cognition.

6. REALITY, DIRECT EXPERIENCED
Knowledge of the Real Through Immediate Cognition

It must be reiterated that the practice of direct cognition through immediate experience is a virtually, unused human capacity. In its place we have developed an indirect manner of understanding that is notionally distanced from the phenomenon. We reason concerning the superficial properties of an object and endeavor to determine what that object is through our own assessment and interpretation. Moreover, we have established preconceived ideas about everything. All the same, neglected is what the object itself may be in terms of its intrinsic particularity, which remains independent of what we think about it and markedly more pertinent than its obvious physical appearance. Needless to say, the intrinsic specificity of a phenomenon is only recognizable through the direct experience of the human, singular distinction.

The indirect nature of the practice of conventional assessment, whether it be intellectual or affective, confines understanding to a limited area and scope that is concerned with the properties of an object but unmindful of what a thing may intrinsically be. Unfortunately, because the cognitive practice of immediate experience remains unfamiliar, the usual circumstantial method is misapplied to dimensions that are beyond its capacity to evaluate. Consequently, indirect assessment suggests that the skillfully analyzed material attributes are the entire extent of the phenomenon, and that quantification epitomizes the entirety of a phenomenon.

In other words, the intellect is incapable of recognizing substantive, intangible distinction, and consequently materialistically established philosophy dismisses physically elusive value in order to preserve the exclusive validity of obvious conditions. The resulting theoretical world-view leans excessively towards the material and entirely neglects intangible qualities, implicit value and the nature of the essential existence of things.

The consequence of defining phenomena solely upon the basis of their physical appearances is the expansion of an abstract, materialistic perspective that is remote from reality because it is confined to conspicuous attributes while neglecting intangible significances. Thereby, the world becomes reduced to a bland counterfeit because an authentic understanding escapes an exclusively materialistic point of view. This would matter less if it were merely the excessive conviction of an extreme minority. Unfortunately, the narrow view of materialism has steadily become a general, human ideology.

A person who only recognizes physical evidence and dismissively overlooks the elusive qualification that inherently identifies phenomena with particular status, establishes a conceptual model at odds with reality. Consequently, a materially biased outlook is bound to be only abstractly pertinent because assessment from an obvious point-of-view will inevitably remain shallow.

In other words, if an investigator establishes an ideology that overlooks profound, intangible significances that are, nevertheless, part of day-to-day experience and justified by human familiarity, then an intentional denial of personal experience has occurred in order to justify a determined viewpoint.

To deny intangible evidence is to neglect substantial data concerning the intrinsic nature of existence in preference for a one-sided theoretical construct. This observational failure is a recognized characteristic of many theories and systems that remain empirically unverified but are nonetheless deemed acceptable and generally adopted because they are well reasoned and seem logically sound. But if acceptance rests solely upon the merits of indirect thinking concerning a phenomenon and the skillful exposition of an argument, confirmation overlooks the immediately determined state of existence of things as they really are, and consequently a significant aspect of reality is neglected. In other words, if a phenomenon is not recognized for what it intrinsically is, but for how we think about it, based solely upon the exhaustively scrutinized, physical properties, our conclusions will be likewise meaninglessly materialistic.

Similarly, every abstractly collated description of a phenomenon remains incomplete because of its remoteness from immediate experience that otherwise reveals the substantive nature. The abbreviated summation is a conceptual substitute for reality because indirect reasoning can only establish an approximate semblance of extant conditions. Conversely, immediate cognition reveals the essential, individual significance and intrinsic nature of things through straightforward engagement.

The conclusions of abstract thinking, established through indirect rationale, will always appear contrived and unreal when compared to immediate cognition because of their remoteness from the actual event. A condition must be directly experienced in order to be thoroughly recognized and authentically known. There is no substitute for the direct knowledge of something, and the constructs of cerebral thinking will always seem strained and alien by comparison.

Immediate experience and subsequent knowledge concerning the immanent state of reality increasingly establish a standard of legitimacy and a sense for the authentic within the sensibilities of the observer.

A contrived notion is immediately identified as such, while merely abstract conjecture and superficial constructs are recognized as inconsonant with the direct view. Consequently, knowledge of the inherent nature of things becomes a significant measure and benchmark against which all other perspective can be instantly tried and assessed in terms of their relationship with the substantive view.

The irony is that conventional, abstract reasoning claims a monopoly of interpretation and an authoritative dominance maintaining a proud conviction of its own infallibility. It derides as subjective and subsequently irrelevant, knowledge established through direct encounter. As it turns out it is the abstraction that is distant from reality while immediate experience is revealed as the final arbiter of authenticity because it knows the nature of the existence of things first hand.

7. TRUE OR FALSE – REAL AND UNREAL
The Importance of the Distinction Between these Terms

It is well recognized that the human intellect is able to postulate, with remarkable flexibility, the merit of any particular statement or chosen position. In terms of that which constitutes reality, the selected benchmark has become the material existence of a phenomenon whereby the scrutiny of the physical properties of something can further, reasonably justify the authenticity of any corresponding object. However, a designation of authenticity that requires unquestionable physicality in order to be justified as real, limits our acceptance to the most superficial consideration.

Through strategic rationale, another abstract position may be antagonistically established that questions the validity of all physical conditions. Through the argument that the human senses are incapable of providing conclusive evidence, the French philosopher René Descartes postulated this approach almost four centuries ago.

A third position, established upon the abstract elaboration of isolated physical propensities as if they had independent existential merit beyond their material context, maintains the existence of an infinity of parallel universes.

These conjectural inferences can be logically and reasonably demonstrated as authentic with enduring conviction so that the non-existence of matter and the prospect of parallel universes continues to be seriously entertained and enthusiastically speculated. Thus, the intellect is recognized for its abstract flexibility while its capacity to definitively determine between reality and fiction remains uncertain.

Ideally, the intellect functions mathematically. Consequently, it is readily able to calculate whether an equation is justified as true, or may be discarded as false. However, as a problem becomes increasingly distanced from mathematical calculation, the infallibility of rationale becomes less certain. For example, it is well known that reason is malleable and in the hands a disreputable or delusional individual, and there are always some who are readily swayed merely by the convincing argument of a proponent. Similarly, our subjectively persuaded feeling-sentient nature may be successfully persuaded that fiction is fact unless our knowledge is established upon an irrefutable benchmark.

True and real; false and unreal, are determinations of validity that have steadily become mutually identified as if there are equivalent. However, there is an enormous difference between what is true and what is real. For example, the aforementioned illustration demonstrates how a postulation may be argued true even though it has no bearing upon reality. Similarly, an argument supporting a philosophical hypothesis may be presented in an extremely convincing way and yet remain merely an abstraction without practical pertinence.

Not only is true incommensurate with real, and false and unreal similarly disproportionate in meaning, but true and false both pertain to abstract assessment, while real is the condition of actual existence that is without converse. In other words, there is no such thing as unreality except as the classification of fiction.

Consequently, we recognize that abstract, rationale concerning that which actually exists is an unreliable, inconclusive exponent through its remoteness from the actual event. Reason calculates, but it cannot directly engage in the manner of immediate cognition. Furthermore, logical deduction must rest upon an initial premise. If a foundational postulate is insufficiently comprehensive, then the conclusions will only apply within a restricted compass.

For example, while, the material substance of a phenomenon undoubtedly demonstrates that something possesses physical existence, it does not follow that the entirety is sufficiently expressed only within corporeal terms. Yet such is the fundamental presumption of materialistic philosophy, and from that sectarian position the authentic nature of existence cannot be discerned because the potential of the existence of anything metaphysical is summarily prohibited.

In reality, all things feature a more profound proportion that modifies the physical appearance with singular distinction, and we know this from our own everyday experience. But the limited perspective of materialistic Western philosophy is a conceptual model that is unable to distinguish intangibles, and consequently, in order to maintain the integrity of a narrow viewpoint, only physical considerations are deemed pertinent.

The real cannot be demonstrated through indirect, abstract reasoning because the real is either authentic or nonexistent. Furthermore, the substantive must be immediately experienced in order to be recognized and conclusive discernment must be made through the infallible agency of the human, essential self.

Actuality is neither a controversial nor a debatable condition. The truth of a position may be established through argument and justified proportionately by sufficiently convincing proof. But reality is recognized through an immediate activity of cognition, not by logical process.

When these distinctions are ignored and reality and truth are considered synonymous with one another, then the difference between abstract reasoning and immediate experience as different cognitive approaches is lost. The result of this confusion is the misapplication of the intellect in an attempt to qualify the existential merit of metaphysical conditions. Consequently, reality is considered established only when demonstrated through a logical sequence of argument. But reality, like qualitative significances cannot be definitively verified through reason.

In other words, intrinsic value and inherent quality cannot be discerned and justified as authentic through argument because they either exist or they do not. They must be approached not through abstract deduction but by being experientially found to exist. Thereby, they are authenticated through direct engagement that is beyond the scope of reason.

In summary, the established, exclusively physical worldview presented by the materialist as *true,* remains a questionable abstraction because it is remotely conceived, independently of the direct knowledge provided by immediate experience. The essential significance of things that is only directly discernible, cannot be dismissed without an extraordinary compromise of perspective. While truth may be promoted through semantic argument, reality has to be directly and conclusively experienced by the human ipseity in order to be clearly recognized and conclusively justified. The human, essential ipseity is the final arbiter as to the real constitution of existence because it views things both directly and impartially, and consequently, through the immediate approach it supersedes the conceptual model.

8. THE PERSPECTIVE OF THE MIND-SELF
The Real and Authentic Recognizes its Own Nature

Conventionally, we recognize two cognitional approaches towards understanding. The one is oblique and indirect while the other is affective and instinctual. However, we also possess a third practice that is inherent to our intrinsic existence. It is both immediate and spontaneous, and it centers upon the human, essential singularity. The direct approach issues from the perspective of our authentic identity. Consequently, it involves an encounter that requires that conjecture and preconception be quieted so that the mind-self may directly meet a situation without cerebral or emotional interference.

The dynamic of immediate cognition reveals through the directness of the experiential approach, not only the intrinsic nature of phenomena but also the significance of the incorporeal, essential singularity of the human observer. That is to say, the mind-self is able to directly experience the authentic condition of existence of an object and simultaneously justifies its own cognitive independence. Consequently, through the activity of immediate cognition, we discover that the human essence is able to objectively encounter its own existence and to recognize the intrinsic status of all other things because both phenomena and the human ipseity occupy essential conditions.

Akin to qualitative significances, the essential, human singularity is recognizable only through direct cognition. Consequently, the singular individuality of the human being is able to discern and know other intangible values, qualities and significances that are consistent with its own intangible condition. In other words, the human, essential identity recognizes the constitutive inherence of phenomena.

While an object of observation can be explored through the conventional approach and be recognized for its physical appearance and the properties derived from its material characteristics, it cannot be known for its intrinsic significance except through direct, experiential encounter. That is to say, in much the same way as the authentic, essential identity of the human being is only known through direct cognition, the intangible, intrinsic identities of all phenomena are similarly determined by immediate experience through the agency of the human quintessence.

The perspectival necessity of the human, essential distinction is of paramount significance if we wish to engage circumstances objectively. Any lesser sense-of-self is necessarily unreliable by virtue of the oblique nature of it's functioning. In other words, for obvious reasons, instinct, affection, rationale and pre-dispositional partiality inhibit immediate cognition.

When the mind-self directly engages a phenomenon, it is able to discover qualitative essentials and the intrinsic significance of the physical that is beyond the capacity of even the most logical thinking to recognize. Consequently, the effectiveness of direct cognition is evident when conventional cognitional processes are restrained so that they may not interfere with the immediate encounter.

The mind-self discovers the intrinsic condition of the existence of a phenomenon through immediate encounter by its own authentic distinction. The intrinsic nature of the knowledge subsequently discerned through direct experience, is inevitable because of the corresponding status of the essential individual and the intrinsicality of the object. It is that distinction that distinguishes the essential human being from the corporeal constitution.

The practice of allowing a phenomenon to reveal its own nature, and essentially identify itself so that the observer may experientially recognize the intrinsic significance, requires a receptive mien. But usually, we are very active in our assessment of phenomena and we are unaccustomed to a passive, cognitional methodology. Nevertheless, in terms of immediate cognition, the approach is not passivity and more an exercise in determined identification. In order to discover the intrinsic nature of something we meet it seeking its particular, existential identification. In other words we inquired as to the designated nomen of the phenomenon, while the answer is revealed through a direct, qualitative experience of its nature.

In other words, the human being almost consistently dwells within an emotional or intellectually abstract mentality. While direct experience seems extraordinary by virtue of its unfamiliarity, nevertheless a phenomenon can be recognized upon the strength of its qualitative authenticity through direct cognition. That which we strive to discover is the dispositional significance of the existence of the phenomenon.

Assessment of the physical properties alone reduces an organism to some kind of mechanical or electrochemical anomaly without intrinsic significance because the exclusive consideration of the blatant, material properties of a phenomenon excludes the qualitative dimension and inherent value. Consequently, in terms of physics, the substances that are most readily determinable are those that are physically measurable and calculable and they are the ones that are exhaustively scrutinized and elevated to represent the entirety of existence.

It is supposed that all phenomena are predominantly physical because we can readily scrutinize and justify the tangible aspects of things. However, if only quantifiable properties are considered, even a living form is reduced only to that which can be calculated or further described in purely technical terms.

But life, in the sense of animation, is not properly explained by the extrapolation of mechanics or chemistry when it is applied to encompass an already living organism. While, mechanics is justified to the degree that it applies to inert matter, nothing comes to life through even the most ingenious mechanisms.

Through materialistic philosophy, the evaluation of a phenomenon is inevitably limited to the accumulation of the physical data concerning it. The assumption follows that the existence of something is entirely physical and consequently, its significance must be similarly attributed. But the influence of exclusive and biased categorization applied indiscriminately, merely means that whatever the perspective motivating the scrutiny of the researcher, the conclusions will be correspondingly of the same kind. In other words, the physical researcher may discover the mechanical motivation of the universe, but we should not for a moment imagine thereby that the entirety is sufficiently explained.

By exclusively studying the superficial properties of phenomena, whether those of a person, animal or an elemental substance, a shallow world-view is established, devoid of meaningful connotations and without the qualitative dimension. When a barren and partial representation is maintained as a comprehensive definition of life, it is predictably viewed with impatience and disdain by those who recognize that intrinsic significances have been summarily dismissed from consideration.

Life, restricted and reduced merely to its tangible properties establishes a mental impasse in the understanding of the researcher that is impossible to rectify through the activity of conventional reasoning. Somewhere the observer must realize that the physical world, devoid of qualitative realities, establishes a bleak misrepresentation without value or significance.

In other words, a materialistic contrivance is established that only exists abstractly in the mind of the investigator, as a ghost of reality. Thereby, exclusive materialism concocts a substitute reality that is essentially futile. That alone should be an indicator to any examiner of integrity that something is very much amiss because it exists in direct defiance to daily human experience.

The discrepancy between the abstract fabrication supposedly representing life and day to day experiential participation would be blatantly obvious if it were not for the conviction that the practice of abstract reasoning founded upon exclusively, materially derived evidence is somehow infallible. In the face of a common and contrary experience that includes substantial and meaningful, intangible qualities, the materialist stubbornly maintains a theoretical and contrived construct.

Cognitional mobility becomes severely restricted when a pre-established structure is allowed to displace our inherent, individual autonomy of apprehension. Reality can only be discovered through immediate experience uninfluenced by preconceptions. While much that is observed and calibrated concerning the physical world is obviously valid, it remains illusory and qualitatively desolate as a definitive determination. By virtue of their qualitative realities, all things are vastly more significant than the mere measurable and calculable parts. A living organism, for example, is alive, and it actually exists. It develops through a cycle of stages, and as an animal, houses a feeling-sentient inherency.

The realization of the actual reality of the existence of the phenomenon of life is a significant event of knowledge. The undeniable fact of the existence of life itself is overlooked and rendered unintelligibly to the cerebral, abstract thinker who is ideally and conspicuously most efficient when dealing purely with amounts and aggregates that can be calculated and subsequently argued. The mechanics and the *how* of cellular functioning may be significantly valid, but compared to the authentic, essential reality of a living form, it is practically irrelevant because the phenomenon is not directly engaged but only abstractly and partially considered.

The mechanics of phenomena are an obvious

aspect of existence, but the intrinsic, qualitative distinction of things is of a more substantive proportion. Consequently, through a narrow speciality, an oblique view of life has arisen that works against meaningful experience and hinders the recognition of essential existence. Further, without immediately experienced engagement, the inherent nature of the existence of a thing will remain elusive and, consequently, our summation of it will be severely inadequate.

The human being has the innate capacity to penetrate to the essential existence and discover the authentic designation of something through the immediate experience of our own individual significance. Thereby, the implication of comprehensive knowledge ascertained through straightforward encounter between the human, essential identity and the equally substantial, intrinsic merit, becomes increasingly feasible with open-mindedness.

Materialism denies the existence of the incorporeal mind-self because it cannot prove its significance through deductive-reasoning founded merely upon physically evident information. Abstraction cannot comprehend that which must be experienced to be recognized. Thus, the materialistic world-view is a severely limited one. But it is less restricted by empirical discipline or serious scholarship and more by the malaise of closed-mindedness to the existence to of anything but blatantly, self-evident tangible properties. Those convinced of a world composed solely of superficial properties will scoff at the challenge to explore the possibility of a more profound capacity of cognition whereby intangible significances can be immediately and experientially apprehended.

The essential, intangible dimension of an object is the reality that endures. For example, upon the examination of a man-made object, both the action of fabrication and the conceptual inception are readily apparent even though they remain intangible. In that sense, the conceptual origin, once realized, remains, even if the object itself is destroyed. One does not recognize the concept if one views the object superficially and merely for its physical properties, nor if the observer already imagines and preconceives an opinion regarding it. If it is already predefined and superficially evaluated then, the conceptual origin will remain obscure. A direct encounter by the human, incorporeal singularity allows us to recognize those enduring, elusive concepts.

The way forward towards cognitional autonomy is the practice of immediate experience through our inherent singularity of existence. Thereby the qualitative significance and essential condition of a phenomenon may be directly discovered. The mind-self and not the intellect become the significant authority of the human constitution. The authentic and substantial nature of the existence of things becomes directly known and, consequently, justified through immediate engagement by the human, essential existence. Thereby, we confront things through imminent engagement and the human being directly experiences the reality of its own existence and therewith the essential and inherent identities of other people and phenomena.

It is vital to further human development that we become familiar with the state wherein the essential significance of things are engaged imminently, and experienced immediately. Reality is a condition of existence that is only discovered through direct experience. It is neither surmised nor indirectly postulated, and it is inapproachable through our conventional cognitive practices.

We have the capacity to know the condition of unequivocal reality for ourselves through the direct attention of our singular identity. An object is observed with the questioning attitude as to what it actually is. However, one does not attempt to answer that question because that would be merely the typical activity of the intellect at work. We engage the phenomenon permitting it to declare its own intrinsic nature.

The human, essential existence recognizes the authenticity of another human being as well as the substantial identity of all other phenomena. The qualitative is recognized by the mind-self without supplementary translation because both entities exist innately. When the substantial existence of another person is directly recognized, as opposed to merely the superficial appearance, the authenticity of their existence is greeted with reverence because the qualitative value of the one recognizes the same in the other. This deference is spiritual love.

Furthermore, the other person is recognized as beyond criticism and evaluation because we encounter their essential existence and find that it is inviolate. Upon the direct cognition by one human being of another, for example, it is profoundly evident that a condemnation of the other is the same as a disparagement of one's own essential self. In that sense, it is similar to a denouncement of virtue.

To encounter the essential identity, which is the authentic condition, is to recognize the intrinsic and innate significance of the human essence. There is nothing mystical about this. It is merely the predictable culmination of the use of the inherent human faculty of immediate experience through the mind-self, whereby all things are immediately experienced for their intrinsic significance.

Any distortion or misrepresentation, falsification or counterfeit is recognized as such because of the capacity of the mind-self to know and differentiate between reality and non-existence or between direct knowledge and merely abstract conjecture. Consequently, it is readily evident when a person has directly encountered the intrinsic significance of things for themselves or if they merely seek to deceive. One is familiar with the reality of one's own self and the significance of other phenomena is similarly evident. A contrived or fictional position is easily recognizable through qualitative comparison.

Further, by practicing the activity of immediate cognition, the qualitative and substantial reality of natural phenomena is revealed whereby objects become known for what they actually are not merely uni-dimensionally. In terms of the interrelationships between human beings, one recognizes the authentic identity of the other and the essential self beyond merely the appearances or particular personality.

9. KNOWLEDGE AND THE mind-self
Exploration of the Human Capacity of Direct Cognition

The actual condition of things is ascertained through objective experience and it cannot be determined in any other way. Actuality is directly discovered through immediate cognitive engagement from the perspective of the human, intrinsic singularity. It is the intrinsic singularity of the human being that ensures that experiential cognition remains objective because the authentic identity of the human being exists not as a corporeal adjunct but elementally and originally. It is through our extant status as a distinctive entity that we are able to originally engage phenomena.

Reason is only capable of indirect allusion because it functions obliquely in the sense that it evaluates conditions not immediately but parenthetically. The immediate experience of a phenomenon reveals its qualitative authenticity, which is the intangible identity that distinguishes it. Without the capacity to definitively determine the difference between the authentic and the non-existent the human being remains within a condition of cognitive bondage.

One would imagine that the conventional practice of deductive reasoning would be a sufficient enough discipline to offer conclusive evidence and thereby enable us to distinguish between the authentic and that which is merely conjectural. Or that a strong faith and assurance, founded upon profound revelation, would suffice. Unfortunately, if the need is for an actual, unequivocal knowledge of the real, neither deductive reasoning nor conviction alone can offer the autonomy of thought necessary to achieve an authentic knowledge concerning intrinsic existence. There has to be a straightforward experiential engagement between the human, essential singularity and the phenomenon, without any other intrusion influencing the directness of the encounter. Thereby, a direct knowledge of the actual condition of the existence of a thing is achieved.

It is difficult to present a convincing argument against the practice of deductive reasoning as a conclusive source of knowledge because it appears to be the best cognitive approach that we have. But every serious thinker is aware of the limit and fallibility of abstract calculation. There are countless theories and hypotheses that are obviously indemonstrable, yet they remain in circulation and continue to be debated. This is because we are unaware of a conclusive, cognitive approach and we must reason and speculate in order to arrive at an equitable conclusion.

Similarly, to suggest that belief and faith are an adequate substitute for autonomously derived knowledge is obviously evasive. One has to be able to find another more appropriate means of cognition that provides definitive intelligence. Fortunately, immediate experience undermines neither of the other practices but qualifies them through a direct knowledge of the intrinsic actuality of the phenomenon. The authentic identity, as opposed to endlessly accumulated information concerning the superficial properties becomes unequivocally known through direct encounter.

It is not difficult to recognize and concede to the inherent limitation and incapacity of logical deduction to achieve definitive knowledge. A mathematical proposition can be flawlessly reasoned by the intellect but not everything can be numerically represented and consequently our understanding becomes prejudiced towards exclusively quantifiable evidence. Further, reason necessarily calculates but, unlike computation, logic is imprecise. However, the candid and principled logician recognizes both the limitations of dialectic and the fallibility of academic consensus.

What terrifies the materialist is the proposition that if rationale is maligned as an approach to knowledge, then faith might subsequently replace reason. Consequently, it becomes necessary to unambiguously distinguish between actuality and the conspicuous vulnerability of knowledge established solely upon belief and faith, even if a creed is augmented by the ostensible authority of revelation.

However, neither philosophy nor faith can deliver definitive knowledge concerning reality because through their oblique approach they are inherently ill-equipped to do so. But the capacity to determine actuality, through direct experience, is a latent inherence within the constitution of every human being. Its usage reveals an autonomy of cognition independent of both abstract constructs and belief.

Deductive reasoning in the search for knowledge or the guileless quest for virtue are obviously valid and commendable endeavors within the boundaries of the aptness of the approach. But the conventional faculties of cognition do not offer a definitive view-point and cannot reveal the intrinsic condition of existence.

Both of the mutually incompatible methods

towards the acquisition of knowledge, the cerebral, materialistic perspective and the approach that requires belief, faith and allegiance to a spiritual point of view, fail to offer cognitional autonomy. The conclusions of the scientific professional must be accepted by the layman with as much belief and faith as is required by the devotee of a religious practice. Both use argument and persuasion to promote their perspectives and both maintain an incomprehensible vernacular decipherable only by the initiate.

That is to say philosophy is clothed in as much mystery and obscurity as the dogmas of the religious, and just as prone to speculative interpretation. They each establish their ideologies concerning the human predicament and the meaning of the world, upon mysterious processes. Furthermore, the extravagant conclusions of the experts, when presented to lay-humanity, slanted through the denial by each, of the perspective of the other, border upon the insane in the light of individual commonsense established upon cumulative life experience. The daunting catalog of emphatically maintained, eccentric assertions and outlandish contentions that have arisen cumulatively through the efforts of the overextension of science, or from religious authority and abstract augmentation, only serve to emphasize the unpredictable nature of both of these practices in our search for meaning.

While many are content with their own convictions, nevertheless there exists a superior manner of cognition that involves the direct approach of the human, intrinsic singularity. It is one that appears strange at first because of its unfamiliarity.

Compounding this difficulty is the requirement that in order to explore the practice one must actually apply it. It can be explained, but it cannot be justified through reason but must be directly experienced in order to be authenticated. Furthermore, it is inaccessible unless we identify with our authentic distinction of our own existence.

However, the true identity of the human constitution, the mind-self is established as the autonomous perspective when the conventional cognitional faculties are constrained. Thereby a phenomenon may be immediately encountered through pure and direct engagement without the interference of preconceptions and sentiment. That being said, the objective is a priceless one and worthy of the work required for its attainment. Furthermore, the perspective presented here is of enormous significance to the future of humanity because it implies the possibility of cognitive autonomy.

10. THE INTRINSIC NATURE
The Essential, Qualitative Reality Explored

The current, increasing lack of wonder and amazement concerning life, is epitomized by the accepted, abstract theories that abound, replacing a direct encounter of reality with a theory or hypothetical construct. These theoretical interpretations have become a substitute for direct apprehension. Thereby, a deductive procedure is followed, and we imagine that we have successfully procured definitive knowledge. Thus, we presently occupy an abstract philosophical condition of our own establishment. This is a predictable consequence of the increasing denial of the significance of the human singularity and our excessive identification with our physical existence. Consequently, if we dismiss the possibility of human, essential significance then we cannot achieve objective knowledge because we deny the agency that makes immediate cognition possible.

The modern materialistic approach contrives a world-view at odds with the common human perception of ubiquitous, intangible significances. The materialist insists, in the face of everyday experience to the contrary, that easily identifiable physical properties represent the exclusive entirety of existence. Thus, an abstract construct is fashioned and maintained that contradicts experiential knowledge.

Consequently, essential and substantial realities, well-known through the empirical training of the artist and by familiar experience during workaday life, are discounted on the grounds that they constitute merely subjective knowledge. Subjectively or not, we know for ourselves that essential qualities exist in their own right because we utilize them in practice. For this reason, we recognize that a philosophy of life that denies the significance of intangible meaning is a contrived interpretation. Additionally, it suggests a further excess from our view because materialism summarily dismisses those essentials that imply qualitative profundity. In other words, physicalism excludes from its assessment of life, all that which is metaphorically presented as significant through the medium of fine art.

The present-day position and practice of specialized, physical research and subsequent philosophical interpretation have isolated investigation from the all-encompassing integrity of life. Consequently, materialistic philosophy has robbed existence of significance, and the observer has lost the sense of wonder.

Direct cognition, through an immediate, experiential encounter with a phenomenon, is significantly effective in removing attention away from the distortion produced by the isolated examination of blatant properties and their theoretical extrapolation. Through explicit involvement, it establishes the attention of the observer upon the object itself and not merely our abstract thinking activity that only indirectly concerns the phenomenon. It leads to an unequivocal knowledge of the intrinsic significance of things whereby intangible, qualitative values are reestablished because through the imminent experience of the human, singular distinction of existence, they can be directly apprehended.

This premise may be eternally expressed and expounded using alternative terminology and description but the vehicle most ideally suited to articulate the maligned and over-looked qualitative realities of existence, is not argument, nor logical justification, but the media and language of art.

The absurdities of an exclusively, cerebral interpretation of life cannot be successfully re-argued using the same terminology of abstract scholarship, but the poetry of life may be recaptured through metaphoric and figurative representation. This positions the testimony of physical exclusivity within a vastly broader, existential perspective.

It is self-evident that experts and specialists in every department, are readily capable of reducing the contrary arguments of the layman to naught through the proficiency of a narrow, professional discipline. But the subject under consideration deals with life itself and the human situation, and it is of vastly too much significance to be relegated and abandoned as the exclusive domain of physicalism.

It is possible to cite the significant works of superior artists as a demonstration of the factual reality and poignant significance of physically elusive existence and thereby reduce the exclusivity of a merely material interpretation of life to a minor reputation. Thereupon, the mechanical world-view increasingly resembles the carapace and fails as a comprehensive explanation of existence because there is obviously more pertaining to life than the material.

Authentic art reminds us of the importance of intangible and incorporeal connotations. Accomplished artwork can reveal the reality of an immediate world of vital and profound human significance. It is a dimension of existence composed of qualitative value, intrinsic identity and the singular, inherent distinction that distinguishes one person from another. While every individual has the innate capacity to immediately experience substantial, intangible realities for themselves, art is the ideal vehicle of their communication.

The essential point concerning the strict limitation of cerebral thinking as the exclusive evaluative approach towards existence, is not resolved through prolonged erudition but may be further clarified through an example of an apperceptive portrayal of the intrinsic identity of a phenomenon, juxtaposed against an intellectual abstraction concerning it that is established upon its obvious material properties. The cognitive recognition of the intrinsic condition of existence of something is revealed by the following exploration of the native element mineral, Iron.

Firstly, Iron will be discussed qualitatively and in detail in order to establish a familiarity with its intrinsic nature, intentionally avoiding the obvious and well established quantifiable properties and conventional classification that have become its formal definition. We are determined to discover what Iron actually is and are less interested in its physical attributes.

Taking a piece of Iron, we wish to describe it to another person who has never set eyes upon it and knows nothing concerning its nature. To offer its elemental symbol, atomic number or its position within the Rockwell scale of hardness is, in this case, unhelpful. We are concerned with what iron is, not its mechanical and chemical properties.

We observe it in the quiet, contemplating without our usual tendency to explain through presupposition, association or sentiment. Our will directs us to encounter the object immediately. The mind-self engages the Iron sample, exploring silently, as if viewing it for the very first time. We allow it to speak as if for itself, independently of our own interpretation. We are endeavoring to discover what it is while examining it without pedantry. The sample is observed in its full three-dimensional state in present timing. Consequently, through direct encounter, it is experientially recognized for the authenticity of its existence and not as we are abstractly accustomed to regarding it. Through immediate experience from the perspective of our own singular distinctiveness we directly encounter the similarly unique, existential condition of the mineral. The full qualitative dimension of its identity becomes evident. It is this intrinsic cast that we endeavor to articulate through the medium of art which, in this case, is metaphorical prose.

The qualitative uniqueness of Iron as a particular variety of metallic substance which, like other metals, can be shaped and molded when hot and cast when molten, lies in its rough malleability and stubborn hardness. It occupies the lowliest station among metals, dumb, common, unrefined and without grace. We know of this through our ordinary experience, but we now strive to articulate what is otherwise denied by the exclusively materialistic perspective. We wish to explore its actual nature through direct cognition.

The metals Iron and, for example, Gold are different interpretations of the same metallic concept of which all metals are alternative variations, yet they each vary enormously in nature and intrinsic distinction. Gold has a quality of rich warmth, while Iron is cold, stark and primitive. Iron is the interpretation of the metal concept as a corruptible dullness while Gold does not tarnish but remains color rich, never losing its imperial luster.

The obdurate materialist insists that qualitative identities are subjective and unjustifiable. Phenomena are classified upon the basis of measurement and calibration because these calculations are readily manageable, intellectually tangible and, consequently, accessible to abstract scrutiny. But the differences between metals are not merely physical. They are essential and distinctly characteristic. They may be subjectively and prejudicially identified, but they also exist as the intrinsic identity that distinguishes one from another.

Both Iron and Gold can be fashioned into the same object but though similarly shaped, the one will correspond as the appropriate metal for the chosen artifact, while the other may seem less congruous. Thus, Iron is ideal for plain utilitarian objects while Gold is ideally shaped for costly adornment and regal symbolism. This is not merely because of the suitability of their physical properties but also their distinct, essential natures befit a certain usage and require an appropriate application. A wedding ring or imperial crown of Iron, would be qualitatively as much an incongruous malapropism as a cooking pot or a garden shovel fashioned of Gold. A crown of Iron would imply a certain cold and ruthless cruelty in the wearer, unlike the majesty suggested by a golden coronet.

The practice of direct observation and immediate

cognition without cerebral distraction and preconception presents an imminent experience of the qualitative significance and intrinsic identity of an object and reveals the nature of its essential singularity. Phenomena are recognized as different qualitative interpretations of general concepts. The metallic mineral concept is a general affiliation that includes all metals. All metals are individual variations according to that same concept. An individual metal, such as Iron is the particular variety of the general, metallic mineral commonality, specifically and distinctly expressed according to conspicuous, qualitative characters.

It may be helpful here to reiterate. The particular variety of the general, metal concept, being examined for its qualitative identity, is Iron. If the Iron sample is observed immediately and not as indirectly considered data, then it is recognized in present timing for what it intrinsically is. Preconceptions, interpretations and sentiment are not allowed to influence the attitude of open-mindedness or detract from direct experience. Through a forthright encounter an object is identified by its intrinsic, qualitative distinction and not merely based upon its obvious physical properties or how we may introspectively evaluate it.

Iron is significantly different from Gold or Copper for its blatant lack of intrinsic warmth. One might arrange the metals accordingly: cold iron, cold silver but less so than iron, warm copper and fiery gold. Similarly, if one were to depict Iron through art colors then the colors would need to be the drab, dull ones. Metaphorically, the disposition of Iron is strong but harsh, numb and grim, obdurate, inflexible and adamant. Iron is tough, rough and severe while Copper is soft and agreeable.

A painting, qualitatively representing Iron would have to portray its cold unyielding nature. The observer, directly experiencing the successful painting would arrive at an experience of that same qualitative distinction that typifies the intrinsic nature of Iron. Yet, the painting hasn't merely symbolically represented it. It would be the same essential quality of iron itself, expressed through an artistic medium.

Nature, character and demeanor remain inaccessible and incomprehensible values to the researcher when only the superficial or physical properties of a phenomenon are considered. But the intangible qualities are nonetheless real and valid, and further establish the authentic identity of the object. But recognized and known only experientially, intangible values are consequently disqualified from materialistic theories that purportedly define existence and have steadily become insinuated into the human mentality as the exclusively acceptable world-view.

Essential, intangible realities cannot be recognized except by direct cognition from the perspective of the individual quintessence of the human entity. To articulate the intrinsic value of a phenomenon is the high mission of art. A drawing or sculpture representing Iron must embody the authentic identity of that particular element and artistically describe the actual manner of its existence.

A pot made of Iron, true to the quality of the metal, must resemble a utilitarian vessel of little grace, squat and open, coarse and rude.

A chalice of Gold, must be majestic, substantial

and fashioned alike to liquid sun. Gold is suitably adorned with compatible gems, such as rubies.

The Silver vessel, finely engraved with the tracery of moonlight, is Gold's handmaiden: a distant, sober reflection of the suns glory.

Similarly, metals may be arranged and qualitatively compared according to their lack of vitality or liveliness. Thus, Lead would occupy a very low position of deadness while dull Iron is less foreboding and so on, through the metals towards fiery Gold.

The musical instruments made of Iron are the dull gong and clanging bell, while those of Silver are more ephemeral: the piccolo and flute in particular.

Iron is of gravity, the core and anchor of the Earth: cold and coarse; the lowliest of metals; utilitarian and base. It is the most simple, crude and basic metallic differentiation of them all. All other metals may be recognized as qualitatively richer and varied in more particular ways according to their inherent nature. Lead, for example, is plastic but poisonous while Iron remains primal and straightforward.

The intellect, slanted by materialistic, Western philosophy, does not recognize the qualitative as equally estimable to the physical appearance but considers it merely a subjective estimation unless, somehow, it can be quantified. We do not seem to realize that subjectiveness merely influences the interpretation of something but does not deny its existence. The intellect is severely mistaken if it dismisses intangible evidence merely because we have not discovered a means to qualify it objectively.

Experiential cognition, through the expediency of

the human, intrinsic identity, objectively engages phenomena because it restrains both the intellect and human feeling-sentience. Its poignant encounter is entirely direct and unalloyed. It is able to achieve this because unlike the intellect the ipseity is not a corporeal faculty but the human, extant entity.

The descriptions of the inherent nature of the metal Iron seem, merely charming. To the intellect they appear as instinctive and inconstant depictions. This is because when a phenomenon is metaphorically represented, it must be recognized through direct re-experience in the condition in which it was initially discovered. But the intellect does not directly experience. Only the mind-self is capable of direct cognition. In order to appreciate an artwork, the intellect must be stilled, thereby an immediate encounter can occur and the essential of the piece may be readily discerned.

When an object is evaluated based upon accumulated, physical data concerning it, it remains only indirectly recognized. The attempt here is to establish that a phenomenon may also be directly known for its intangible significance. The sovereign individuality of the human being is able to confront the object of interest without the intermediary of cerebral thinking or of sentiment. It draws from the phenomena a knowledge of the inherent identity and the intrinsic significance of its existence. It identifies the object for what it authentically is.

Thus, the metal Iron is discovered for its real identity and not merely classified according to its physical properties. While furthermore, the intrinsic distinction between metals is not established merely upon their appearance or how we feel about them, but on their inherent identities.

The conscious, human individuality discovers the essential identity of the phenomenon through direct encounter because substantively, the inherent nature of the object and the incorporeal, conscious individuality of the human being are of an alike original existence. That is, the inherent identity of the object is also incorporeal and it is this qualitative reality that we strive to identify and articulate.

Iron

Neath mountain fortress, caverns deep
Slumbering giant of the keep
Sightless gaze and brooding mien
Primal, Earthbound, grim, unseen.

Slow of wit and thick of tongue
Tamed by fire, hammer-song
Shackled now to masters will
Captive from beneath the hill.

Furnace fury, pounded, drawn.
Molten Iron wrought and formed.
Spark a flying from the boil
Fire and forge transform the soil.

Attendant on the bloody field,
The Iron servant does not yield.
Crushed and broken, scattered, cast,

Dull and servile to the last.

Unlike Silver, Iron mute
Never praised by harp nor flute.
Hollow clang, coarse of phrase
Iron dull 'gainst silvern praise.

No Iron trinket gained a lover's heart.
Better shod to heel or cart.
No devotion won with dreary token,
Nor passion deep through Iron spoken.

From halls of yore, Iron ore,
Cavern, furnace and rust once more.
Yet, within that dense and witless plight
Mysterious magic comes to light.

Dull, stalwart Iron, plain, phlegmatic,
Cohorts with current and becomes magnetic.
Without pretense, nor affection,
The gravitas of Iron is Earth's foundation.

By Julian Hamer

    The bolt shown above is manufactured of Iron and, additionally, it embodies the conceptual origin of its fabrication. That origin remains intangible, yet it is recognized through its condition as the fabricated bolt.

    Thus Iron, itself owns intrinsic distinction that can be explored and identified through immediate cognition, but the bolt also embodies conceptual causation that is similarly recognized through immediate encounter by the human, singularity of existence.

    Every construction and structure are possessed of conceptual origin. Without conceptual origin, things exist elementally but without particular arrangement.

11. THE AUTHORITY OF THE HUMAN mind-self
mind-self Cognition Applied to Nature

A compound of materialistic theories defining life, founded upon the conviction that everything consists merely of matter and energy is at odds with experience. Abstractly, these constructs make reasonable sense but fail in practice because they exclude intangible, qualitative values that are otherwise universally known through human experience.

A theoretical interpretation of life void of intangible values, nuances of quality, character and demeanor, is an unreal and contrived distortion that contradicts common knowledge. However, it is strongly held conviction, so much so that if the materialist begrudgingly concedes to the authenticity of incorporeal value and to the significance of qualitative subtleties, they are assumed to be physically generated even though they are directly known to be otherwise.

In other words, the established theory is formulating the research. This perspective is typical of the adamant theorists who construct structures and systems inside their heads oblivious of what is actually going on, and through a determined partiality, dismiss challenging data merely because it is of a different texture.

It is unfortunate that the materialist remains convinced of something that fails miserably when compared to everyday life. But this subterfuge is achieved by avoiding direct experience and consistently interpreting everything in exclusively abstract and superficial terms. It is further perplexing when incorporeal values are defensively dismissed while the materialistically exclusive construct is upheld in the face of direct, opposite experience because such is an indicator of zealotry and less of openminded thinking.

While abstractly conceived theoretical concepts, that reduce all things merely to anonymous material building blocks and energy, are convincingly argued they remain compelling only as an artifice. One becomes impatient with theoretical schemes, systems and abstract contrivances and alarmed at the insistence of their supposed mathematical infallibility. It is disconcerting to recognize that we are not thereby dealing with reality but merely belief systems, certainly of a sophisticated composition, but otherwise alike to any other. The fault lies with an almost complete ignorance of the practice of human cognition through immediate experience, further exacerbated by nescience that insists that only the calculating intellect has the capacity to definitively evaluate circumstances.

Cognition through immediate experience reveals the significance of non-material values. It does so through direct encounter of the physical and not by intellectual interpretation which is by its very nature abstract and indirect. Beginning with one's own self, certain qualitative realities become known. Experienced through first-hand encounter they become self-evident and their authenticity is upheld through a direct cognition between the recognized actuality of the human being and the object of immediate interest.

The paramount authority of the human being is the singular distinction of our existence but it is usually distracted by the workings of the intellect and feeling-sentience. But the authentic identity lies not in our corporeal faculties and subjective feeling nature nor within personality, capricious emotional preferences or somehow ephemerally as a mystical concept. The identity and prerogative of the human being resides within the authentic individuality, which is the mind-self.

The mind-self is the only viable and justified identification of the individual. All else is transitory. The human mind-self recognizes its existence through immediate experience, as an incorporeal and constant reality. This recognition provokes an experience of astonishment at the phenomenal authenticity of one's own individual self. That one's own existence should be discovered directly and known as a reality is found to be an incredible insight that is only further evidence when the ipseity thereby discovers similar essential significance appertaining to all other things.

Furthermore, experiential knowledge of the authentic, individual reality of one's own self further reveals the incorporeality of immediate existence. Consequently, upon the direct experience of the phenomenon of our intrinsic singularity, we find that we no longer identify with the body as our distinctiveness because reliance upon conventional perception is suspended so that the essential may be experienced first hand. Thereby, the innate significances of things discovered through direct cognition are found to be quite otherwise than the obvious, physical appearance.

The conscious, human individuality, whose attention is directed through respective will, always recognizes a phenomenon afresh. This is because the human essence confronts a situation immediately without reference to associated recollections. The mind-self always experiences an object as if for the first time because it does not entertain preconceptions.

Accordingly, the superficial, conventional human identity is set aside in order that the intrinsic existence might be directly known through immediate experience. The enduring significance of people and phenomena cannot be otherwise ascertained. Similarly, the indirect, abstract manner of reasoning is superseded by direct cognition and the essential identity of all things is experienced through an immediate encounter by the mind-self. That is to say, to the degree that cerebral activity and subjective feelings are restrained in order that they may not obstruct or distort direct cognition, the intrinsic significance of things becomes evident through first hand knowledge.

The human mind-self is of a different nature than biological corruptibility. It endures beyond physical circumstances and the bodily requirements of sustenance for growth and survival. Therefore, it is entirely distinguishable from biological transience, and its existence remains unquantifiable and incomprehensible through physical scrutiny and mathematical analysis.

The existence of the human, essential distinction is determined solely through immediate, experiential engagement, and known only through direct encounter. Consequently, the significance of the mind-self is justified directly through pragmatic knowledge and the straightforward experience of its own existence. Furthermore, the perspective of the mind-self towards all other phenomena, reveals a correspondence between the experientially known, incorporeal and unique individuality and the substantive and enduring qualitative content comprising the intrinsic condition of things. It is the human mind-self that discerns and identifies the elemental condition and particular nature of things, that otherwise can only be obliquely surmised through our conventional, cognitive faculties.

Abstractly, through intellectual deduction, one can only determine properties that are coherent to the calculating rationale of conventional thinking. The mind-self is not of the same substance as the reasoning nature nor does it require the intellect in order to justify its own existence. It is an explicit entity that is discovered directly through experience because only the intrinsic human identity can discern unequivocal conditions. The human, singular distinction exists independently of corporeal constraints, and consequently cognition is always direct, immediate and experiential.

It is the task of every moment to reverse one's attention from a corporeally established view, and cultivate the authority of the mind-self. However, this is a self-perpetuating activity because the experiential knowledge of immediate existence is of itself, tremendously stimulating and liberating. Furthermore, concerning the perspective of the human, essential identity, nothing abstract nor cerebral can approach or compare to an immediate experience of the intrinsic significance of things, while subsequent knowledge concerning their actual condition makes certain that there is no going back to the former, peripheral prospect.

This is immediately evident and readily recognizable by the individual who has discovered through immediate experience their own singular existence. It is also blatantly obvious when another assert such knowledge, but has not attained it. The gaze of the mind-self readily differentiates the superficial and abstract from immediately experienced knowledge. It is the difference between the profound and the indirectly conceived, or the authentic view through actual knowledge rather than mere belief, conviction or theory. The one is actually how things are while the other is oblique perception. This is self-evident to whomever authentically experiences essential existence through direct cognition.

One cannot definitively determine the essential nature and identity of a phenomenon through abstract reasoning because it requires a direct and instant engagement with the object itself in order to know its intrinsic condition. Furthermore, the practice of immediate experience and subsequent knowledge reveals the world to be profoundly vivid and meaningful because the substantive dimension of things becomes evident through essential discernment.

Abstract reasoning, void of the experiential directness of the human ipseity, seeks to project its intellectual and materialistic deductions, attempting to define the sensible world within those narrow terms based solely upon the shallow appearance of things. However, methodical abstract deduction is conventionally considered the highest achievement of human cognition. The resulting philosophy claims exclusive authority in this regard, through ostensible successes achieved by exhaustive analytical argument and qualification that is further supported by peer consensus.

This poor substitute for immediate engagement is established upon the abstract justification of an exclusive material view. But it is revealed as a slender counterfeit of reality from the perspective of the mind-self. Consequently, when existence is immediately experienced, the abstractly deduced construct is found to be inadequate because phenomena are reduced to meaninglessness when solely evaluated upon the perfunctory, material appearance.

In the sense of understanding the entire significance of things, the material alone, however painstakingly scrutinized, represents only a partial view. Overlooked is the intrinsic significance of the existence of phenomena. However, directly ascertained knowledge reveals a far greater depth of relevance than is physically apparent and establishes an unshakable standard and benchmark against which the many and diverse professions of comprehensive knowledge may be evaluated.

The mind-self exists as an emphatic entity that discovers itself through direct experience. Its unique significance cannot be ascertained or justified by deductive process and argument, nor maintained as valid through consensus. In other words, if the researcher solely considers material conditions to be significant, the essential distinction of things necessarily remains elusive. That is, the existence of physically elusive situations cannot be verified from a specifically material point-of-view. Thereby, a paradox is constructed if an exclusively physical, philosophical worldview is maintained because the mind is closed to the discovery of the substantive proportion of things if the means of its identification are denied by a narrow ideology.

Ideally, conventional thinking seeks to reduce all

things, including living organisms, to their component properties in order that they may be rendered more intellectually manageable. When a phenomenon is reduced to *numerical* terms it is most perfectly suited to deduction because it may be calculated as clearly and succinctly as mathematics. The exclusively physical approach maintains those extracted values as the solely valid definition of a phenomenon, because they can be readily rationalized. Thereupon, superficial properties are examined and scrutinized to an ever decreasing scale of minuteness in an attempt to discover the genesis of the whole.

It is believed, that with increased reduction, fundamental building blocks will be discovered and the material world successfully interpreted. But the scrutiny of physical properties, encouraged by the abstract concept of rudimentary building blocks, does not reveal the essential nor the authentic identification of a phenomenon.

In other words, the qualitative value and intrinsic distinction of a thing cannot be discovered solely through an examination of its material attributes because essential significance is integral to the whole and does not exist outwardly in the consequences.

The examination of physical appearances indicates and reveals how a thing functions according to physical law but intrinsic distinction cannot be similarly deduced. If we wish to know how something works, we must ask the engineer. But mechanics can never determine what an object inherently signifies, but it will describe the existence of a thing in the purely functional terms.

The essential distinction of something exists incorporeally as the authentic identification epitomized by the intrinsic quality and particular nature of its existence. Consequently, integral nomination can only be acknowledged through those human faculties that can recognize similarly qualitative, intangible significances. While physical attributes only partially correspond to the nature of the existence of a phenomenon, the elemental pertinence of something can never be found in the sum of the physical properties because the original, substantial distinction of the whole is lost through analysis.

As an example, conventionally, all insects are recognized as arthropods by their general similarities. The singular identity of any one variety is classified exclusively by its physical appearance. Yet, the qualitative nature of expression and not the physical difference between two insects reveals the distinct and intrinsic identity.

According to George Crabb, (English Synonyms 1816), *The quality is that which is inherent in a thing and coexistent; the property is that which belongs to it for the time being. We cannot alter the quality of a thing without altering the whole thing; but we may give or take away properties from bodies at pleasure, without entirely destroying their identities.*

The distinction here is between quality as the identity that is discernible only through immediate experience, and properties that are the tangible features.

The qualitative distinction is the experientially known integral relevance that we described earlier. In terms of the insect world, obviously the dragonfly and the mantid are both insects that possess different appearances that are readily identifiable. But each insect species expresses an inherent qualitative nature that differentiates one from another in terms of what they are as alternative expressions of the general insect concept. That is to say, the properties and distinguishing features are not the inherent nature of the creature. The inherent nature is expressed consistently throughout the intrinsic, qualitative characterization of the particular insect.

The physical parts, as Mr. Crabb explains, can be removed without altering the essential, inherent identity of the creature. The wing of a dragonfly can be removed, but the insect still remains a dragonfly. But if the intrinsic nature of the creature should somehow change then it would be an entirely different insect expression with an accordingly altered physical appearance. It is this incorporeal, integral nomination that becomes known through the direct application of the attention of the human mind-self. Conventionally, merely the external properties are conceded while the qualitative distinction remains unidentified.

An understanding of the difference between qualitative natures as opposed to physical properties contains the entire significance of organic form variation. The differences between creatures lie in their essential, qualitative distinction and not solely upon their physical appearances.

Lyudmila N. Trut is head of the research group at the Institute of Cytology and Genetics of the Siberian Department of the Russian Academy of Sciences. Her work has grown out of the interests and ideas of the late director of the institute, the geneticist Dmitry K. Belyaev. (Early Canid Domestication: The Farm-Fox Experiment.

American Scientist, Volume 87).

Half a century of Fox breeding revealed convincing evidence of a significant correlation between the dispositional temperament of the fox and its form. As the captured wild foxes became tamer and more adjusted to human interaction through many generations and, consequently, were selected for breeding upon the basis of agreeable temperament, they also began to develop subsequent form alterations. These changes included curly tails and tail wagging, floppy ears, piebald coloring, and snouts that tended to be shorter and wider.

The foxes were not chosen and bred for their physical properties but for an increasingly amenable temperament and tame-ability that made them easier to manage. Consequently, over time, a gentler disposition developed and increased among some of them through a direct interaction with humans. As the selections continued upon that basis over many generations of foxes, alterations in physical form became significantly more apparent and consistent. The general physiological relaxation from wild, snarling beast to pleasant pet with a colorful coat, floppy ears and curling tail was the reciprocal correspondence to a developing amiability and amity of character. The intentionally encouraged, pleasant disposition was most effective when human interaction occurred at a very early age. Significantly, both the new physical traits and the improved disposition were hereditary.

The work at the institute unequivocally demonstrated that when creatures are selected and bred for their altered temperamental qualities the form appearance will correspond accordingly to that intrinsic change in disposition. In other words, the nature of a creature is composed exclusively of intangible characters and temperaments. Consequently, the quality of the physical properties must correspond with the essential disposition of the animal. Thus, the creature is most accurately identified according to its intrinsic character which is its incorporeal identity, and not conversely by its physical properties.

The intrinsic nature is the descriptive identity of a phenomenon that influences the physiological presentation. The physical characteristics of the insect or of the fox are not the intrinsic identity but the consequences of the character of the particular temperament. That is to say, the quality of the form appearance corresponds with the nature of the essential, intangible disposition.

12. OPEN-MINDED OBSERVATION
The Avian Concept

Unless one views an object with a completely open mind, as if observing it for the very first time, it is unlikely that the phenomenon will be apprehended in its original state. Rather, it will be evaluated and classified according to our own existing preconceptions, prejudices, or superficially from an examination of its superficial appearance.

Open-mindedness is required in order to discover the authentic state of things without misconstrual through prejudgment and conventional association. One has to assume that one does not know anything and consider the object of observation from an attitude of ignorance. Open-mindedness is essential to the activity of immediate cognition because conventional evaluation will otherwise hinder the direct encounter and obscure pristine, experiential engagement.

In order to gain knowledge through direct engagement with a phenomenon, the mind-self must be permitted to encounter the object without interference from prior assessment and recollection. In other words, the mind-self must be able to engage the object immediately because it is the human, unique entity alone that has the capacity to achieve imminent, experiential engagement and thereby discover the essential significance of things.

Examining a bird feather one recognizes that it is the realization of a distinctly pertinent response to the avian condition. Just as the eye is entirely and perfectly established as an organ appropriate to light and of the quality, nature and character of light, so the feather is entirely respondent of the essential quality of the air.

If the eye were not entirely predisposed to light and appropriately fashioned according to the quality and intrinsic nature of light, it would be without optical value. If it were less than immaculate, it would cease to effectively serve the organism. Thus, we recognize and establish that the physiological circumstances of an organism are dependent upon the nature of the ecological context. In the example of the eye, we recognize that the form and operation are entirely predisposed towards the constitutional nature of light.

While the eye is correctly regarded as an immaculate light organ, the wing and the unified avian construction must be similarly recognized for its comprehensive affinity with the air and of aerial flight.

The fin of the fish and its entire composition is fittingly and appropriately an organic extension of its watery milieu. The fish is of the water as the eye is of light and the feather is, likewise, distinctly aeriform.

That is to say, the fin of the fish is moot without the ocean to swim in. The eye is irrelevant without sunlight, and the avian concept is meaningless without air.

Being of the air presents an array and complexity of completely different constraints and conditions than those of the terrestrial or aquatic creatures. There is nothing arbitrary in the composition and structure of a feather. It is entirely suited to the avian ambiance and fitting in every way for successful and dexterous, aerial mastery. The bird of the air is as nimble in flight as the fish in the ocean or the earthbound creatures in their own particular element.

A feather is a flight resource of immaculate and supremely successful, living construction and organization. Just as the pull of gravity effects the composition and structure of earthbound creatures and the buoyancy of water is of enormous significance to the build and constitution of marine animals, so the avian is similarly composed according to the bidding and requirements of the air. The downward strain of gravity is contradicted throughout its structure in order to emancipate the creature of heaviness and provide it with aerial dexterity.

In defiance of the influences and demands of gravity, the feather is entirely suited to the properties and motions of the air. The creature that takes to the air is constituted of a corresponding nature to that medium. The dependence of the living creature, to the attributes of the air and corresponding mastery of flight, suggest that the qualitative nature of the aero-sphere and that of the bird are perfectly pertinent to one another. Thus the correspondence between air and the structure of the creature, like that of light and the immaculately composed eye organ, necessitates that the form adheres completely, throughout its entire composition, to the ambiance and essential quality of air. It is as if the air milieu dictated the architecture of the creature according to its own nature.

The conditions, restraints and laws of flight, while external to the organic prototype, just as light is external to the eye, require scrupulous, structural accommodation by the creature in order that the avian may thrive in that very exacting medium.

It is asserted and determinedly defended, that variations in the forms of creatures arise by chance and caprice, and eventually, over vast ages, through natural selection produce living forms of a condition that is suitable for flight. It is imagined that the capacity of flight arose by chance from an arboreal ancestor and subsequently progressed to the eventual survival of an avian strain.

Immediate observation of the feather reveals the perfect unity and correspondence between the quality of the aeronautical form of the bird and the essence and constitution of the aerial medium. The feather of every bird of flight is an immaculate aeriform structure. The air medium necessitates that the entire bird composition conforms to the stringent demands imposed by its intrinsic condition and quality.

The concept of spontaneous and capricious variations that arise for no reason to be sorted for advantage by unprompted opportunity fails in many ways. When a creature is restricted as a particular animal then variations in form are only possible within the scope of that creature's definition. Thus, a bird cannot arise from an arboreal creature if that animal is already restricted to a certain, form specialty. The avian progenitor would have launched itself into flight from a far more generalized, form condition that already held within it the potential of flight.

The attainment of a certain structure must be already contained within the progenitor, as potential. Thus, the animalian antecedent must have possessed universal prospects that existed in unrestricted and undefined condition in order that they might extend according to the specific propensities of the creature. Consequently, we must imagine not an endless succession of already specialized creatures but an undefined primogenitor of unlimited, improvisational flexibility.

Becoming aerial was a niche occupation by an indeterminate form, provoked through ecological circumstances that were radically different from our familiar constraints. An undefined form has the capacity to specialize, but the already specialized creature may only alter within the scope of its differentiation. The idea of a gradual evolution from already defined forms into differently, specialized creatures does not address the perfection of ecological adaption.

The primordial bird must have flown through the ancient tree tops with as much grace as it does today. The concept of flight could have never been achieved in a piece-meal fashion because partial, form alteration is not the same as the capacity to fly. Further, there is no advantage in a condition that is incomplete, and therefore even the abstract theory of spontaneous anomaly fails to explain the development of flight. Established in part, the creature would have, necessarily, remain unsuccessful.

The aeriform construction of the bird is an entire and immaculately comprehensive expression enabling the creature to dwell at ease within the wind, the currents and to even feed in flight. It is not a partial nor halting correspondence but one that is ecologically reciprocal and consistent to all birds. Thus, the avian could not have arisen from the lizard but would have developed from an archetypal ancestor that possessed the potential to develop in either direction according to the particular animalian penchant and predilection towards diverse, ecological challenge.

There are countless varieties of birds, each characteristically distinct in the way of form and plumage, but with every one, the avian principle remains consistent as a standard of viability and overall composition. Every individual bird is a variation of the general affinity of the animal towards flight. The same harmony is entirely represented throughout the bodily structure, and further realized in particular ways that are markedly different according to the influence of the particular, compounded, temperamental propensity of the species.

The avian commonality includes an affinity and compatibility of structure that is consistent with aerial life. Those birds that have forsaken flight remain distinctly avian even while embodying terrestrial qualities and physical characteristics for activities such as sprinting, burrowing and the conspicuous aquatic properties of waterfowl, including the penguin whose wings are flawlessly reapplied and used as flippers.

Similarly, the eye always remains of the nature of light even when reduced in size and altered in structure for the convenience of the tiny insect. The eye remains optically viable and true to the essential nature of light as a general eye concept. Likewise, the avian concept remains the consistent reality of structure for all birds. That birds difference in appearance is attributable to continued feeling-sentient adaption towards ecological challenge. This provokes an adjustment of nature that effects a consequent alteration in appearance within the parameters and confines of the existing form. It is here that so-called Natural Selection occurs as a minor, capricious adjunct.

The avian condition itself is greater than all bird variations because it remains general while the variations are specific and particular interpretations. However, the avian precedence would be of even greater universality, represented as a vertebral archetype, while the expansive biology of insect and botanical forms could be traced in detail to the same organic principles.

A bird of a certain nature and demeanor is the specific and characteristic interpretation of the avian, true to principle, yet, expressed according to its particular temperament. Thus, the differences between two birds are cumulative, characteristic distinctions according to the manner and disposition in which the creature's respective natures express themselves.

The identification of specific, qualitative variations of a general concept or principle such as the avian, is an unusual view. However, when one observes creatures in present timing and with open-mindedness, it is self-evident that this is indeed the reality. Listening to the calls and signals of creatures reveals very different manners and peculiarities of expression. While, for example, the comparison of the warning cries of different birds leads to an appreciation of the qualitative variations between them.

Animals inhabit the world of feeling and all of their sounds and behaviors are founded upon a temperamental constitution. They do not strongly reason, but they investigate and question from a sensibility of mood and disposition of instinctual feeling. As feeling-sentient creatures, the particular and predominant demeanor of a bird indicates the manner in which the avian concept is specifically interpreted.

Firstly, a living creature must function flawlessly as an organism. The biological integrity of operation can never be compromised. Consequently, individual varieties must always adhere consistently to the requirements of structure that allow them to remain viable, living creatures because if a creature fails to maintain natural integrity, it perishes.

The avian concept is in a dependent correspondence with the air just as the eye corresponds in structure with the nature of light. The nature, and consequent appearance of a creature, as demonstrated through the Russian fox experiments, is established by its qualitative response to a compound and accumulative ecology.

There is nothing random nor arbitrary in the architecture of the feather. Flight is not achieved in half-measures. It is either entirely successful or an abject failure. The medium of air would have no patience with trial and error. The bird has to be exclusively and perfectly aerodynamic. It always remains entirely successful and appropriate even when represented by multitudinous variations. The concept of the feather and the entire avian constitution is immaculate. Dexterity in the air is exacting and avian ease and facility demonstrates a very precise respect and deference to its demands, epitomized in form and expressed in almost endless variation, yet, always viable and true to the general demands of an ambient ecology.

Thus, the archetypal progenitor was necessarily both immaculate and fully functioning. Creatures did not evolve from simplicity but diversified according to their particular and changing temperamental responses to a diverse ecology. Meanwhile, their qualitative distinction and disposition influenced the appearance of the form accordingly.

13. FROM UNDEFINED TO SPECIFIC
The Manner Whereby an Overall, Governing Principle is Variously Interpreted

Over time, the knowledgeable woodworker becomes very familiar with particular wood characteristics, and respects the individual distinctions that markedly differentiate the species. Furthermore, beyond the obvious physical properties, a craftsman will recognize the essential character, and consequently respect the significance of those intangible subtleties. For example, if woods are compatible and of a type, they will work well together and enhance the composition of a piece. But some combinations conflict and must be used cautiously and employed with those disparities of character in mind.

Obviously, we can learn a great deal concerning the general characteristics and the intrinsic nature of a particular wood from a study of the tree itself. One type of tree thrives in a cold region while another will flourish only in the tropics. One requires considerable moisture while a different species will perish with too much rain. In the climate of arid desert, a tree of a certain character survives but would otherwise fail in the far northern regions of the tundra. Furthermore, while evergreen softwoods abundantly populate high altitudes and colder climes, the deciduous varieties increase as the mountains give way to lower level valleys and spreading plains.

Clearly the tree genus, as a general botanical classification, is expressed differently and more fittingly depending on the particular ecology to which it is most suited. This includes acidic or alkaline soils, the mineral composition of the earth and well-drained or water-logged terrain. In other words, a particular species of tree will only thrive where the ecology is ideally congruous to its specific nature. In this sense, a tree can be said to possess inherent temperament.

The general or ideal expression of a certain tree represents a standard according to which a particular character of vegetation must comply in order to be recognized and considered authentic to type. The overall general criterion of all vegetation concerns photosynthesis and the tree is a more specific definition within that general description. The manner whereby the ideal principle of the tree is particularly expressed constitutes the dispositional nature whereby the general, is specifically represented. The particular nature of a tree and the idiosyncratic interpretation of the tree type are synonymous. That is to say, the type is the idiosyncratic quality of expression according to which a primordially developed standard is explicitly realized.

The familiar tree expression developed anciently in a particular, characteristic way because of the unavoidable constraints that certain ecologies demanded of a more flexible, indeterminate vegetation. Furthermore, general vegetation become increasingly specified through the idiosyncratic specification of certain dispositional proclivities that are the essential nature of the tree. However, character does not change incrementally, but the overall temper of expression modulates and acquiesces responsively within the available limitations and latitudes of feasibility. In other words, in order to thrive optimally within a changing ecology, the predisposition of the species must correspond qualitatively with the environment.

As every arborist knows, an ecological dynamic exists between the intrinsic nature or character of a particular tree species and its optimum environmental situation. Everywhere, there exists a tension between the dispositional nature of the tree and the insistent ecological constraints and characteristic attributes of a certain locale, as well as the influences of the greater ecology. However, in our day, peculiarities of expression are no longer flexible except within very narrow parameters, and if considerable mismatching occurs, the tree will perish because a cumulatively established disposition has long since become predetermined and no longer possess the necessary potential to devolve.

In other words, characteristic differences, induced by a diverse ecology upon an earlier less specified expression of the tree standard, have developed into very distinct interpretations so that the particular tree has become strongly associated to an ideal ecology with which it has compromised over time through an adjustment of its constitutional nature.

In a sense, the comprehensive environmental context provokes the general expression of the tree to conform according to the ecological character. A further reciprocal dynamic includes environmental changes that are caused by particular trees that eventually influence and shape their own surroundings. Meanwhile, those trees themselves are required to additionally adjust in character, in a sense, to their own influence.

Different trees have become strongly appropriate to some environmental circumstances over others so that domestic trees, when planted in foreign soil must be treated with respect to shade or sunlight, water, soil quality and even the companionship of other trees. Few trees, for example, thrive in the immediate neighborhood of the walnut.

Further adjustments that arise as variations in subsequent generations, are only very slight alterations to an already established nature. However, there is no longer any such thing as an unspecified tree. Long ago the non-specific character was altered and modified according to a particular nature, and while some present modification may continue to occur, it can only happen within the limited terms of an already specified expression.

To reiterate, present day trees no longer embody the potential to revert to the former general nature of a progenitor because they have become otherwise defined and the ancestral ambiguousness no longer exists. The severely defined form, therefore, becomes adapted to a very specific ecology and change can only transpire within the parameters of an established nature. In other words, the extant tree is acutely vulnerable towards ecological change in a way in which the ancient, undefined progenitor was not. This efectively, is the substance of Dollo's Law of irreversibility. (Belgian paleontologist, Louis Dollo. 1893).

The original, unspecified form no longer exists. Hence, there is no going back to an earlier undifferentiated character because that general expression has become long since superseded by the development of a specific nature. The acacia cannot become an oak because both trees are distinct and there no exists longer a general potential within the acacia to become the very distinct oak. There is nothing in the existing nature that is uncharacterized and could become something else that it does not presently embody. The acacia might become vaguely more oak-like under peculiar circumstances but it could only ever be a slightly oak-like variation of the acacia nature and never an authentic oak. Each tree has become almost entirely specific and has the capacity to alter only within the scope of that specificity. Natural variations are, therefore, only very superficial.

The tree is a collective expression of a type of vegetation. The differences between expressions of the tree concept are qualitative. The acacia and the oak are trees of an entirely different quality of interpretation; each characteristically established according a long biographical challenge within a shifting ecology.

The ecological dynamic between the tree and its environment is also a qualitative one. While superficial properties may be scrutinized, the identity is not in the details but in the compound nature of the entirety. The complete expression of a characteristic nature does not develop through the piece-meal appearance of isolated traits, but the entire nature assumes a qualitative tenor that is represented throughout its composition. It is this intangible nature that is the true identity. The difference between two tree representations lies in their characteristic interpretation whereby each entire tree is expressed according to its own nature. Thus, one finds in the nature of the tree, an intangible, qualitative identity that may be artistically referred to as its characteristic motif.

The motif is the essential nature of a particular tree variation whereby its distinction is accordingly expressed. It remains incorporeal as the authentic identity or the manner in which the tree concept is subsequently interpreted.

Superficially, the tree is defined by the particular properties of seed, flower, leaf and trunk. Yet, all theses parts are expressed according to the character of the tree which is the real, although incorporeal, identity. These properties are the tangible expressions of a singular, intangible nature. They remain the exhaustive and comprehensive expressions of a distinct nature-motif whether they appear as seed or flower, leaf or trunk. Thus, alterations in form that arise, reside, initially, within the nature-motif or overall character of the tree and not in the apparent adaption of separate properties. The entirety is the only thing that can change, and the identity of the entirety is the intangible nature of the tree, upon which, the interpretation of every aspect, remains contingent.

If one observes the acacia and the oak for their qualitative differences, it becomes evident that the characteristic motif of each is the nature whereby the standard definition of the tree is optimally expressed in a specific ecological context with all its various constraints and demands. The particular interpretation of the tree concept is the qualitative realization of a dynamic between the ecology and the particular nature of the tree. It is because the essential nature or characteristic motif of the tree is its real identity and in a way, mirrors a specific ecological context, that a tree fails to thrive in an inclement climate. In other words, the nature of the tree and its ecology correspond qualitatively according to a cumulative process of adaption.

To know a tree one must discover its comprehensive nature and articulate the characteristic motif. The difference in the characteristic motif of two trees can be described as a certain propensity or disposition towards one direction of expression or another. The depiction of a tree in qualitative terms is recognized as its most effective description. Once again, qualitative natures are most effectively expressed and communicated through the language of art.

Traditional Chinese calligraphy, in particular, beautifully epitomizes the essential dynamic between the intrinsic nature of the tree and its particular ecology. The influence of the ecology upon the nature of the tree is continuous. Eventually, the tree appears almost as an extension of its aboriginal context.

Yet, to claim that one tree has a different personality to another would be to anthropomorphize and, in a sense, trivialize the differences in the characteristic motifs that are the essential identity of a particular interpretation of the tree concept and the reason for its particular appearance and behavior. That trees exhibit different and characteristic qualities, there is no doubt, some being aggressive propagators and fast growers while others are recognized as slow, steady and enduring. The traditional woodworker chose an appropriate wood, from a particular part of a tree because of its nature, some lumber being suitable for one purpose while another variety is ideal for a different application.

A violin, for example, would be an absurd instrument constructed of oak, while a garden tool handle made of hickory is entirely appropriate.

An excerpt from the book, *Longitude*, by Dava Sobel, 1995, illustrates this point:

Aside from the fact that the great John Harrison built it, the clock claims uniqueness for another singular feature: It is constructed almost entirely from wood. This is a carpenter's clock, with oak wheels and boxwood axles connected and impelled by small amounts of brass and steel. Harrison, ever practical and resourceful, took what materials came to hand and handled them well. The wooden teeth of the wheels never snapped off with normal wear but defied destruction by their design, which let them draw strength from the grain pattern of the mighty oak.

Harrison's clock had bearings of lignum vitae, a wood so dense and hard that it readily sinks in water. It is also self-lubricating. Thus, the character and nature of lignum vitae, as opposed to pine, for example, is readily recognizable for its qualitative properties. But it is not merely identified by its hardness and its closed grain, density, resistance to wear and abrasion or the lack of distortion through moisture variations. These are physical properties. The wood is correctly identified by the quality of its expression, while all the material conditions necessarily correspond to that original nature.

One searches for qualities of expression first. A grasp of the essential nature will reveal the manner whereby every aspect of the tree is similarly expressed. Thus, the leaf, flower, sap, trunk and quality of wood are all direct expressions of the one character but within different areas of the entirety of the composition. The same, singular motif is always expressed throughout.

14. THE ESSENTIAL IDENTITY
Superficial Properties and Qualitative, Intrinsic Significance

The superficial appearance and the inherent identity and significance of a phenomenon, are recognized as essentially distinguished from one another through the intrinsic human capacity to differentiate between the appearance and the essential, through immediate cognition. Inherent significances can only be directly discerned and experientially known. Consequently, a reasoned assessment founded upon the appearance of something may be logically valid yet remain, essentially, malapropos.

The interpretation of a phenomenon or an event is typically and conventionally founded upon prior experience or assessed from the perspective of a certain mind-set, belief or scholarship. Frequently, a conclusion is predictable depending on the particular approach, underlying convictions and preconceptions. For that reason, a thing is seldom engaged directly and originally, and recognized for the intrinsic nature of its existence.

Furthermore, an original and direct encounter through the aegis of the human, unique singularity, immediately demonstrates that our usual cognitional practice is sadly shallow and thereby we overlook the full significance. The problem is, intellectual or emotional supposition, founded solely upon the conspicuous state of things fails to achieve a knowledge of the intrinsic significance. Formally, everything was understood through myriad, associated preconceptions and sentimental biases but phenomena were seldom fully engaged and identified for their essential condition.

An examination of the difference between two interpretations of the same thing, one material and the other essential, reveals the qualitative significance as vastly more meaningful than was formerly supposed.

The human capacity to discern and identify a thing for its authenticity, remains latent and undeveloped. Usually, an observation and subsequent evaluation are determined to be valid to the degree that the assessment is qualified by sound argument and a position is fortified through knowledgeable consensus. The particular parlance of the frame of reference ensures the consideration of a novel approach. Consequently, the exploration of a position stands more upon an acceptable vernacular and not necessarily because it is definitively demonstrated as authentic.

What is required is a disciplined practice of observation whereby the conventional and customary approaches are superseded by a manner of discernment that penetrates to the crux and essential significance of a phenomenon or situation.

A phenomenon must remain uncompromised and unclouded by intellectual abstraction and subjective emotion in order that it can be experienced in its original condition. In other words, direct encounter through the conscious, individual self is that latent capacity of discernment.

The difference between immediate cognition and oblique interpretation through the intellect or feeling nature is a qualitative one. Direct engagement reveals the intangible value of a thing while conventional cognition involves the status of peripheral properties.

Consequently, reasoned interpretation will always lack the authority of intelligence that is acquired through immediate experience. That is to say, the qualitative difference between phenomena must always be directly ascertained. Otherwise understanding remains uncertain because of the inevitably, oblique perspective of indirect, intellectual and emotional evaluation. In short, the physical properties comprise the cursory appearances that are the easily, assessed features but they do not necessarily indicate the authentic condition of the existence of something.

    For example, as we explored in the last chapter, we experience a tree through direct cognition and recognize that every detail embodies the authentic nature. It is according to this nature that the entire tree and all of its aspects, are expressed. It is this characteristic nature of the tree that determines its identity. Every feature, detail and attribute of a tree are expressed qualitatively according to its essential character. Therefore, the tree is entirely comprehensive and consistent of nature throughout.

    Thus, the theory of arbitrary variations, winnowed by natural selection, is not significantly supported. Whereas the existence of a distinct, cumulative nature in reciprocal dynamic with a specific ecology is very much reinforced by immediate observation.

    The particular nature of a tree is an interpretation of the general tree concept, adjusted cumulatively according to the demands of an ecology that may vary considerably over time. It is through variations in character or nature that the material form tends to express differently in appearance and it does so, not in the isolated detail, but comprehensively. The form becomes differently interpreted because the characteristic nature whereby it is expressed has altered in response to a change in the ecology. It is these adjustments that appear as inconsistent, physical traits that may be naturally or intentionally selected. Indeed, when we look at phenomena from the perspective of the nature of their expression, we understand the proceedings all the better.

It is in this regard that the difference between the conventional emphasis upon the physical properties of an organic form, as opposed to the inherent quality and identity, becomes clear. A scrutiny of the superficial appearance does not lead to a knowledge of the essential nature. Yet, an immediate grasp of the inherent, qualitative identity, through direct cognition, explains the particular appearance.

The tree remains comprehensively and qualitatively of the same characteristic nature throughout its entire structure. The pine cone, for example, is recognized as the same, qualitatively, as the bark or branching system. A pine needle remains authentic in nature to the inherent, qualitative identity of the particular variety of tree, now expressed in the form of foliage. The appearance of the parts differs yet, the particular tree interpretation must still remain faithful throughout to the inherent and particular quality of the variety.

That is to say, the comprehensively expressed nature of the particular variety of tree remains consistent while the appearance of the feature necessarily alters in metamorphic juxtaposition, depending on its position within the ideal conceptualization that is common to all vegetation.

A variety is a specific interpretation of an ideal concept. This ideal was classically known as the archetype. Every tree, in order to remain viable, must adhere to the archetype that generally summarizes a functioning arbor. This requires that the particular, qualitative identity of the tree should metamorphose throughout the physiognomy of the entirety, expressing through the same nature, the leaf, bark or seed. The type must still viably conform to the ideal tree concept while remaining consistently true to its nature.

The ideal concept of the tree or the archetype is intangible yet recognizable through its application. Like the qualitative inherence that determines the particular tree variety, both exist elusively but they are recognized through their function.

In other words, every tree remains true to principle while expressed individually according to the particular qualitative nature. However, both archetype and particular nature exist as intangible realities that may only be recognized through immediate cognition. That is, through direct experience by the unique individuality of the human being.

It is important to establish a personal understanding of organic life by contemplating it originally and directly with an open mind rather than referring to an established, conceptual model and seeking to validate and qualify an abstract position. Once introduced, the model becomes stubbornly entrenched and difficult to challenge even though we claim to recognize that a hypothesis is only a convenient and even temporary construct.

Increasingly, through the support of technical sophistication, materialism is becoming the entrenched perspective towards existence at the expense of intangible value. With the enhanced use of refined equipment and computer modeling another layer of abstraction is established that represents a further disengagement between the researcher and the phenomenon. Thereby, popular concepts become reinforced by the use of instrumentation designed to augment a preconceived assumption by calibrating or manipulating a property as if its conclusive identity were recognized and already definitively identified.

This dissociation is an unfortunate development because it is through immediacy that the inherent condition of phenomena is determined and through the agency of the intrinsic, human self that the full dimensionality of existence is apprehended.

When the reality and the fact of the existence of living phenomena is grasped, not as a pre-established, conceptual construct, but through immediate encounter, and the materialistic yearning for a tidy mechanistic interpretation is relinquished, knowledge arises as a personal experience through immediate cognition.

Direct experience provides knowledge of the characteristic nature of essential significances because it is achieved face-to-face without any intermediary evaluation. The attention is moved away from abstract constructs and conjecture and, accordingly, the substantive becomes immediately known.

All manner of fiction may seem reasonable and justifiable to the mind that is unsupported by an immediate experiential knowledge of reality. A mind unaccustomed to immediate, experiential knowledge, will be blown every which way by convincingly presented arguments and the popular, theoretical speculation of the moment.

Immediately determined knowledge is far from mysterious. It is merely unfamiliar and consequently it is treated with suspicion. Direct engagement seems to be an incomprehensible cognitive device if understanding does not arise through familiar intellectual activity.

Nevertheless, direct cognition originates through the mind-self when the reasoning mind is quieted and the intrinsic person becomes the direct observer. Thus, there remains no separation between the incident and beholder and the ipseity can encounter the phenomenon immediately, in present time. It is solely through the mind-self that direct knowledge is achievable because, as an entity, the human, singular distinction alone is able to experience phenomena directly and objectively.

15. LIFEFORMS
Viable, Organic Organization and the Agencies of Life

Every individual human being has the capacity to determine the essential significance of things through immediate experience and to explore the intrinsic nature of phenomena through direct cognition. If we directly examine an egg or a leaf, without the misguidance of conventional interpretation, an affinity towards the elemental relevance of phenomena is established against which abstract conjecture will always be found insufficient and seem hollow.

The phenomenon of vitality may be determined by its presence and be further qualified by its absence. A living form observed beside a dead one reveals a profound, qualitative disparity. The effect of vitality is the maintenance of living continuity. Life continues as long as the form remains viable. Viability requires that the form remain intact and workable so that it may successfully flourish in accordance with the ideal principles that establish a working organism. However, while the organic form must remain a tenable one in order for vitality to animate it, that alone is not enough. It also, of necessity, requires directly or indirectly, the presence of the four, quickening agencies that facilitate animation.

A flowering tulip, restricted to the shadows, will twist and writhe in search of sunlight while at night it will close its petals to darkness and await the new dawn. If this phenomenon is observed straightforwardly, it will be recognized that sunlight is composed of a quality that is indispensable to plant life. Although the tulip has no optical eye, the whole aboveground plant seeks sunlight as if, in its entirety, the plant were an organ of perception.

The same is true of water. The roots of a tree will search relentlessly for water, some reaching depths of eighty feet or more. Similarly, the needles of a cactus are the leaves reduced to a minimum surface area so that the plant may not lose moisture in a severely, arid environment.

In Springtime, the warmth of the sun signals the seed to awaken from its contracted sleep, unfold and increase to its mature reproductive stature. But, in order to thrive, the seed must be moist and the plant must have warmth, air and sunlight. Thus, sunlight, water, air and warmth must be recognized as quickening agencies.

In other words, an organism only remains vital under specific terms. Naturally, it must continue to be structurally viable in accordance with the ideal concept that ensures that it may function, and somehow it must always include the presence of the life supporting agencies of air, moisture, warmth and light. Thus, it will thrive continuously throughout its particular lifecycle, through every metamorphic stage of expression.

The plant's predisposition to propagation likewise remains with the undamaged seed as long as the seed continues uncompromised and tenable. In other words, vitality does not capriciously abandon a sound organic organization during dormancy but as soon as the invigorating agencies are available proliferation begins anew. Thus, upon the occurrence of the stimulating resources of the quickening agencies, the organism awakens, ingesting its appropriate nutrition, whether it be healthy soil or other organic forms that it may ingest and transmute to its constructive advantage.

To reiterate in other words, vitality is essential to the physical realization of organic organization. A creature ceases to exist without it. But it only animates structure if the organization and integrity remain sound, otherwise it abandons a form when that system becomes unfeasible and fails to retain a tenable structure. The structure of an organism must remain intact in order that the quickening agencies may be able to sustain it. Vitality will not countenance a compromised organic form but, conversely, vivifies a viable form consistently. It animates a form ceaselessly throughout all its metamorphic appearances and continues on through the seed. When that organic system is challenged through an adverse ecology, the character of the creature must either appropriately conform and adjust to accommodate the threat to its viability or die away whereupon nothing can bring it back to life.

Simply put, life continues as an organic continuum as long as the form remains tenable and the quickening agencies are present. If the organism breaks and can no longer operate, it is forsaken and life-forces alone cannot rebuild it. Conversely, the creature also fails if the quickening agencies are missing. In other words, a pristine archetypal organism remains viable conjointly with the quickening agencies and would always have to have existed accordingly in intimate combination.

There is no organic animation without the successful complexity of a viable organization. Life sustains that organization perpetually but it abandons individual, unworkable forms, wherever the particular organization is compromised. The seed is the most contracted condition of an organism. It is the complete and inherent identity of the form in its most physically intense form. Vitality remains regardless of the metamorphic appearance but growth and propagation require the catalyst of the quickening agencies.

In short, the vitality of the quickening agencies, together with tenable, organic organization, remain within a consistent dynamic. Present must always be a complete organism for vitality to animate and the agencies of life must also be active. Never can there have been a state or condition when this was not the reality. The agencies of life sustain organic organization but when the creature is compromised, vitality cannot reanimate it. Similarly, the archetypal, organic concept cannot be physically consummated without the attendant agencies of life.

The search for the essential basis of organic life within inanimate matter is fruitless. Vitality is inconceivable unless there is continuous, functional organization sustained by the agencies. When such an arrangement exists, then vitality is likewise present. But without organic order there is nothing for life to animate. Consequently, there must always have been the animated subject and vitality together. Vitality does not spontaneously arise unless a working, organic structure is concurrently extant. On the other hand, life remains imminent as the vivacity of air, water, warmth and sunlight, but extraneous without intimate affiliation with an organism.

The essential requirement for animate life is a viable, organic organization true to an ideal, workable concept. The ideal of organic organization or the archetype is the ambient conceptual structure that is, subsequently, qualitatively and particularly interpreted as a variety of expression or species. The life supporting agencies and essential nourishment, whereby the organization takes earthly substances and transforms them into bio-material for its sustenance, must be similarly apparent. When the form ceases to comply with the ideal concept which is its essential working integrity, or is denied access to the quickening agencies, it becomes compromised and vitality can no longer sustain it.

There is no such organic organization within the mineral kingdom. The mineral condition is the inanimate state into which organized, organic form descends when it ceases to function. It is a state of disorganization containing no compelling arrangement to vivify. The mineral kingdom is the graveyard of disintegrated, organic organization and contains nothing that the agencies of life can animate. Coal, oil and chalk were all once upon a time organic. Nothing can revitalize them except indirectly when the organic, life organization itself transmutes the inanimate minerals into biochemicals. Otherwise, they remain dead.

Thus, the theoretical construct that suggests that organic life arose from the mineral kingdom is untenable. Wherever there is organized and viable organic form and the quickening agencies of life, there will be simultaneous vivification. Where no such organization exists, there is no vitality. Organic organization and vitality always occur simultaneously and continue in tandem perpetually until the organization itself is compromised through degeneration or by the absence of the sustaining agencies of life.

Recognition of the nature of animation can be immediately discerned through the comparison already introduced at the beginning of this section. A living form is compared to the lifeless phenomenon and its lack of vitality is starkly revealed. The absence of the same is equally obvious when the organic form disintegrates. If vitality is absent, it cannot spontaneously arise. It is self-evident that there is no viable organic structure to be found anywhere in the mineral kingdom that vitality can promote and sustain. Organic organization must exist because life forms are a continuum but life cannot accidentally arise from inanimate and inconceivable conditions.

Without vitrifiable organization, physical law remains irrelevant. Law is not the instigator nor the promoter of vitality and neither is it capable of conceptualization. To attribute life to impartial physical law is similar to the search for the origins of life in the mineral kingdom. Yet, modern physics maintain the contrary. It endeavors to discover the source of organic life where no animated organization exists.

The physicist attributes life and organic organization to material laws where, in reality, law is nonproductive. Forces are an aspect of the comprehensive, ecological conditions that impact the appearances and the manner of functioning of organic life, but physical law is only influential, not causal. Natural criteria are the array of situational specifications and conditions that determine how an organism performs and how it appears. If osmosis were somehow different or the pull downwards of gravity were less, then, all organic life would appear and behave otherwise than we now know it. But these conditions are not originally formative.

Every living organization corresponds intrinsically to a particular ecological situation. A bird is an aerodynamically, immaculate creature and cannot be conceived of without the acknowledgment of an intimacy between form and the quality of air. Organic forms adjust and alter to comply with the compound, ecological constraints, challenges and laws and retain viability by adaption. Adaptations are adjustments to the characteristic manner whereby the ideal concept to which the variety belongs, is locally realized.

The poet-scientist Johann, Wolfgang von Goethe (1749 – 1832) described this natural dynamic as a dynamic of tension and its reconciliation.

Tension indicates a restraint or challenge to the viability of the organic form through ecological circumstances. The living organism must resolve the threat through the adaption of the qualitative manner whereby it interprets the ideal, working principle that it exemplifies. Thrown a vital challenge, a plant or animal will reorganize its characteristic nature in order to ameliorate the imminent hazard. However, by now flora and fauna have become severely restricted through prior, cumulative adaption so that their present range of options is much reduced and severely limited. In other words, the significant compromise of the characteristic nature is considerably less available to most creatures than formerly when their forms were less specific and unspecialized. When a challenge is slight then a variation of nature arises and, concurrently, there may be a successful behavioral alteration. When the challenge is too severe, then the organism dies.

16. THE IDEAL CONCEPT
The Realization of the Archetype

Theoretically, through the restrictive deception of sophisticated instrumentation and the analysis of readily quantifiable attributes, organic matter may be assumed to be reducible even to an electrical event. But an electrical event has no organic organization that the agencies of life can vivify and there is no such thing as a living partial-constitution.

This is self-evident to immediate experience. Every part remains authentic to a particular entirety because it is an aspect of the manner in which the specific phenomenon is expressed and every aspect is of the same characteristic nature as the whole. An integral part of the entirety remains qualitatively true to the particular expression that is comprehensively and thoroughly expressed throughout. Thus, in terms of inorganic chemistry, a sulphate is always qualitatively true to the particular element with which it is bonded. Similarly, every property of an organic form remains faithful to the quality, essential nature and identity of the particular creature.

No aspect is separate from the intangible character and demeanor of the whole. Everything retains the same value and essential identity as that of the entirety. Accordingly, all aspects of a whole are the same qualitative expressions even in difference local contexts within the entirety and are, correspondingly, true to the particular nature.

The condition of elemental intrinsicality, engaged through immediate experience, reveals the existence of essential, incorporeal and ideal patterns upon which all separate and individual organic expressions are realized. Those concepts comprise the archetypal viability of the organic form. The form must remain authentic to the principles of the ideal but, as in music, where many variations upon a theme may be expressed, so also, it is the same in nature. Yet, those variations must remain faithful, in principle, to the original concept in order to remain viable.

The notion has developed, as a result of an exclusively materialistic, abstract perspective towards existence, that infinitely small and uniform building blocks of matter have somehow coalesced into order and, subsequently, come to life. They remain miraculously coalescent, fully functional and reproductive while they progress to further complexity through spontaneous mutation that is winnowed for advantage through Natural Selection.

In reality, the order and arrangement that organisms assume, reveals the presence of intangible, archetypal principles. Every organic form has to remain authentic to a conceptual paradigm in order to remain feasible. Everything living has to maintain the integrity of completeness. Therefore, the completeness of an entity resides in its adherence to the essential exemplar, according to which every variation must remain consistent and true, in order to exist. There is no such thing as an incomplete, living organization or of nondescript parts that then arbitrarily coalesce to establish a complex singularity.

Anonymous parts do not authenticate the integrity of the whole because all aspects of the entirety are necessarily of the same nature. There is no such thing as matter without identity. When an electrical event is recorded and maintained to be the minutest reduction of matter, in reality, it merely reveals the presence of an electrical event of a certain nature and not an anonymous, material foundation.

Physicists imagine that matter may be almost infinitely reduced until it is no longer material but exists as a *God-Particle* which is an insubstantial event, determined merely as a flash in the pan. In reality, matter possesses particular, elemental identity, and incorporeal, conceptual standards comprise all organic organization, without which there would be no life.

The materialist will claim that the existence of an archetype is a mere belief, like any other, or an abstraction. Their dismissal and ridicule rests not upon empirically derived information but merely a defensive knee-jerk reaction against something unfamiliar. However, through immediately ascertained knowledge, conceptual structures are self-evidently recognizable realities and belief has nothing whatever to do with their authenticity. The intellect evaluates, judges, and chooses, imagining that the authenticity of existence is deducible while, in fact, it can only be known through immediate experience. Knowledge of reality is only possible in present timing and is only discovered through direct encounter.

The archetypal paradigm of vegetation, for example, while realized through infinite interpretation and variety, remains, of itself, a discernible reality to direct cognition. Every variant must remain consistently true to the conceptual arrangement in order to be practical and workable. A partial or incomplete organization is consequently unrealistic. Similarly, in the mineral world, the allotropes of carbon such as graphite and the diamond, remain true to a common substance while differing enormously in appearance. However, the disparity in aspect is primarily conditional upon the innate, qualitative distinction whereby each is expressed.

The realization that all organisms must remain authentic in principle to an exemplar, in spite of their particular variations of expression, suggests an already extant conceptual foundation that is the inaugural incentive of organic form. Further, as stated above, the quickening agencies that vivify organic organization must exist and must have always existed simultaneously with the organism.

Similarly, the metamorphic stages of the insect through a cycle of different appearances reveal an individual insect variety, alternatively realized. The qualitative identity is retained throughout form change and every aspect and detail remain authentic to type. In fact, every appearance remains intrinsically the same, although metamorphically transposed and consequently different in appearance, according to the demands of the general concept. Thus, the egg, the caterpillar, the chrysalis and the butterfly are all exactly the same nature of creature in alternative guises. Recognizing this as the authentic state of things enables the observer to realize how something thoroughly authentic, such as an intrinsic identity, can at the same time, exist intangibly.

To reiterate, there resides essentially an archetypal exemplification according to which an organic form must comply. The archetype alone assures viability as the working ideal. Therefore, the creature only functions and sustains life as long as it remains true to the archetype. While there is an infinitude of qualitative variations that are provoked by the compound ecological context in which the animal or plant finds itself, the effective principles remain consistent. Meanwhile, the ecological context incites the creature to adapt, which it does qualitatively. In other words, the archetype endures because therein lies functionality, but the manner of expression alters and consequently changes the physical emphasis and tenor of the creature-type. That is, the expression changes reactively in character and demeanor in relation to ecological demands and challenges.

There are two distinct criteria that determine the appearance of a living form. The one is the archetypal paradigm while the other is the qualitative distinction. Thus, a variety of tree remains consistent in principle to the archetype. It must do so, or it could no longer function and sustain vitality. However, the particular tree variation substantiates a specific character-demeanor of interpretation which is the essential motif whereby every detail and aspect remains true to character throughout the form. Thus, nested, we have the concept and the nature whereby it is practically realized. Together they determine the appearance of an organic form.

The archetype of the tree is essentially an incorporeal, conceptual arrangement that is never purely realized except in principle. The archetypal exemplification remains the viable ideal. But when realized organically it is expressed according to a particular, qualitative interpretation that is provoked through the ecological context. The cumulatively refined, qualitative variation becomes increasingly distinct and speciated.

Every tree is composed throughout of the same, living substance that is transposed metamorphically depending upon its particular position within the entirety, according to the demands of the archetypal pattern. The living substance is throughout, always consistently of the same qualitative character. Thus, we recognized how every single cell of an organic organization is identified as having identical DNA.

The archetype is qualitatively and characteristically expressed as a particular distinction. The qualitative manner is epitomized throughout every detail of an organism and may be suitably characterized as the motif of expression. The motif is physically revealed as the subject or theme of the organic expression.

Both the archetypal paradigm of living organization and the qualitative nature whereby it is physically realized are intangible realities. Intangible significances are only reluctantly condoned by materialistic Western philosophy because they can only be justified by implication or through subjective experience. However, they are directly encountered and objectively recognized through immediate cognition by the human, singular distinction.

17. A QUALITATIVE EXAMINATION
Sunlight, Color and Darkness

Sunlight may be known for its qualitative nature most readily through the direct observation of the colors revealed through a glass prism. It will be recognized that the colors are extremely vivid. It is as if one were observing living light. If the quality of the spectrum of daylight is compared to electrical light such as that produced by a G.E.D. it will be easily recognizable that they are of a different character. The G.E.D. light, through whatever colored filter, remains spectral and unnatural. It is a qualitatively cold light something of the nature of the electric arc or of the laser.

Sunlight can be characterized only with great difficulty by direct observation. But observed through a prism or seen as a spectrum side by side with electrical illumination for comparison, its quality is readily discernible. The vividness of the colors has already been mentioned but they are further qualified when it is recognized that sunlight is one of the principle agencies of life. Sunlight possesses the inherence of vivification and promotes life in living organisms.

Increasing familiarity with the quality of sunlight revealed through a comparative study of the colors of the prism spectrum, enables us to recognize the same character of vitality in other phenomena. It will be recognized that the color quality of living vegetation from the greens and browns of trunks and foliage, the blossoms and flowers and the colorful fruits of the garden as well as the rich colors of tiny insects and sea creatures that directly absorb sunlight, all possess the same vivid quality. Indeed, so does firewood burning in the hearth.

Further observation of the spectrum of sunlight reveals a transition between the colors. They are both distinctly separate and they pass through a progression from one color to the next. Similarly, in Nature, the colors of vegetation develop in a manner that frequently corresponds to the contracted or expansive nature of their forms. This is particularly dramatic in the progression from one metamorphic form such as the stem of a flower, through the sepal, the petals and the reproductive organs. The intensity of color becomes increasingly vital with contraction and less intense with expansion. The expansive colors are qualitatively different from the contracted ones. Furthermore, the transition between the colors can be seen as correspondingly abrupt upon condensation or gradually progressive as the color spreads.

The vitality that sunlight bestows directly upon organic life is revealed in their appearances through a quality of color that is unequivocally akin to that of sunlight itself. That is to say, the vivacity of sunlight is revealed and re-echoed it the nature of the coloring of organic life. While, plants grown hydroponically under artificial condition appear strongly green, nevertheless, they seem somehow unwell. Comparing the two phenomena, we discern a strong distinction. Sunlight is wholesome, while electrical lighting is essentially noxious.

Qualitatively, sunlight is recognized as an agency of vitality but from the perspective of materialistic scientific opinion it is considered to be the result of the radioactive, destructive disintegration of matter. However, by considering phenomena merely upon the strength of certain physically perceptible properties they become classified exclusively in technical terms. The qualitative is scarcely recognized at all and therefore the phenomenon is consistently misinterpreted through the exclusive examination of physically derived information. For example, if we consider the previous example concerning natural and artificial light, we understand how light may appear similar upon the calibration of extrinsic properties, but entirely differently when qualitatively compared.

In other words, sunlight possesses significant qualitative value which is its intangible connotation and authentic identity. We have come to recognize sunlight merely as physical energy because we cannot determine any other material substance. Sunlight is undoubtedly energetic, but it is not merely electro-magnetic.

The qualitative significance of sunlight is revealed through the exploration of the circumstances of different natures of sunlight illumination. The physical constitution transforms as heat through absorption, while the essential significance reveals the qualitative warmth that the fine artist yearns to portray. Thereby, two starkly different dimensions are discernible within a single phenomenon. Thus, sunlight possesses two of the vital agencies essential to organic existence but beyond light and warmth remains a wholesome, qualitative eminence. These different natures reveal an astonishingly multifaceted phenomenon that cannot possibly be represented merely as a mathematical equation.

However, while for convenience a light source may be calibrated through the numerical terms of brightness and color, the interaction between sunlight and a tangible object, immediately reveals qualitative distinctions. A color pigment will change in appearance depending on the vigor of the sunlight to which it is exposed. In darkness a tree has only black coloring. The light at dawn illumines it, and the colors appear and change with the rising sun throughout the day. Sunlight constantly changes the appearance of an object according to its brightness and how it is diffused by the Earth's atmosphere.

Thus, during the day, under varied conditions and, in different seasons, sunlight varies in quality. Consequently, the color of pigmented objects and their shadows alter correspondingly as daylight differs in character.

Similarly, if moon-light is observed through the prism and its spectrum is examined it becomes readily apparent that the quality of moonlight is as vivid as sunlight. But moonlight does not produce warmth. The technical interpretation of this measured in angstroms is a far cry from the qualitative expression of the artist. The calibration is an almost meaningless description that does not remotely approach the immediate experience of the actual phenomenon.

Consequently, once more we find that quantified, physical properties fail to express the essential quality of the reality. Those who remain within an abstract, oblique mindset that exclusively consider phenomena understood upon the strength of a superficial basis, scarcely know reality at all except remotely, in abstract terms.

Nevertheless, the moon is bathed in the vitality of sunlight but remains organically lifeless, being void of the other agencies that sustain life-forms such as water and air, and lacking viable, life organization. The addition of the other agencies alone would not revitalize the moon into a green satellite because simultaneously, along with the agencies of life, must exist contiguous and living organization in order that those same essential operatives can animate and vitalize.

The moon is sterile and incapable of rejuvenation but as it reflects sunlight it reveals something of its own nature mirrored in the silvery hue. In other words, just as color pigment is illumined and revealed alternatively by the different qualities of sunlight upon the Earth so the quality of the moonlight is also expressed through a pearly wash that illumines Earthly objects in its own distinctive way.

Silver (Moonlight)

Slowly, silently, now the moon
Walks the night in her silver shoon;
This way, and that, she peers, and sees
Silver fruit upon silver trees;
One by one the casements catch
Her beams beneath the silvery thatch;
Couched in his kennel, like a log,
With paws of silver sleeps the dog;
From their shadowy cote the white breasts peep
Of doves in silver feathered sleep
A harvest mouse goes scampering by,
With silver claws, and silver eye;
And moveless fish in the water gleam,
By silver reeds in a silver stream.

Walter de la Mare

Sunlight, seen through the needles of a pine tree, sparkles with rainbow colors. This diffusion of sunlight reduces its intensity and it illuminates decreasingly through color, towards the black shadow beneath the needles, which is finally no light at all. Diffusion is not the same as hindrance through an increasing thickness of filters but the scattering of light through reflection and refraction. The surfaces of the pine needles distort light in all directions while the glass prism does so depending upon the orientation of its reflective planes. Diffusion alters the illuminative quality of light.

The artist who articulates an elusive subject in the language of color, can use those different qualities to suggest a mood associated to a time of day, geographical location or seasonal changes. Thus, a human portrait, painted as if with the colors of Northern European winter, will express a completely different disposition than the same portrait composed of colors typical to the light of a Southern Italian summer.

The qualitative nature of the declining intensity of sunlight upon a snowy landscape is artistically portrayed by the German poet Goethe. It is a description achieved through immediately experienced observation, void of abstract deduction and analysis. Sunlight is neither measured nor calibrated, nor removed from the actual context, and certainly not intellectualized. It is depicted neither as photon nor wave but as a waning presence in the snowy landscape. In that natural vista, the chromatic diffusion of sunlight into color occurs until, suddenly, darkness reasserts it prerogative.

In illustration, if one observes objects outdoors through a glass prism, it is readily apparent that the color spectrum inhabits the transition between sunlight and shadow. Upon the border of every shadow, between sunlight and along the edges of objects, the spectrum of colors is evident. Red progresses towards the sun and indigo towards the shadow. Thus, the prism serves to diffuse sunlight in a controlled and concentrated manner and reveals progressive coloring between light and shade. There is less color spectrum observable in the shadows themselves unless dappled sunlight has crept in. Indeed, even without the prism the color transition between sunlight and shadow still exists, but it is only noticeable, with difficulty, and under ideal circumstances.

Color pigment is also not the same as sunlight. The spinning-spectrum color wheel that appears gray-white is incommensurable with sunlight colors. This is demonstrated when theater lighting gels of the same colors as the spectrum wheel, are held together against a sunlight source and reveal not gray-white, but black. The spinning-spectrum color wheel is a fabricated experiment that demonstrates only the visual experience of blurred, color pigmentation.

Sound allows the hearer to experience a phenomenon from a distance. One can know the quality of a source through a direct experience of the sound itself. Every sound has a particular qualitative identity. One learns of the intrinsic nature of the origin of the sound through immediate apprehension. Sound can be experienced immediately without identification and interpretation.

Likewise, sunlight can also be known without connecting it to a preconceived idea. Sunlight is an experience of the quality of the sun, but at a distance. Yet a direct experience of sunlight reveals the quality and nature of its source.

When one recognizes the phenomenon of sunlight by its vitality and as an agency of life and notices the manner in which it transforms into heat, a grasp of its essential nature begins to become established. It becomes possible to know sunlight as it in fact is and not merely by its apparent properties. Sunlight is essentially life-giving.

Qualitatively, the substance of the sun is sunlight. We know the quality of sunlight directly and experientially because it is here and we dwell corporeally within it upon Earth. We know it qualitatively and immediately through our own direct knowledge. Only if a material object obstructs sunlight does light become warmth. Therefore, ideally, sunlight is heatless unless obstructed by matter, and invisible unless physically mediated. That is, when entirely uninterrupted and unhindered, sunlight is without color and without heat. That is to say, although the circumstances of sunlight may differ, the intrinsic nature of it remains a consistent, qualitative identity.

In short, sunlight can pass through a vacuum because, like darkness, it has no material substance. Unlike warmth or sound, it does not require a medium of transference. Warmth requires a conductor but sunlight does not. Sunlight can transfer through the vacuum of space, from the sun to the Earth in the form of light but not as heat. Sunlight is non-material, yet when light is hindered by an object it transforms into warmth. Sunlight, therefore, can also be described as latent warmth. Sun warmth has a most distinct quality that is quite unlike, for example, electrical heat.

Sunlight, as warmth and as light, are both essential to organic vitality. Sunlight may be qualitatively described as life-promoting and its warmth as life-enhancing. Sunlight and sun-warmth are qualitatively distinguishable by distinctly different influences.

Striving to allocate material properties to sunlight, solely in terms of energy causes the qualitative reality to be overlooked, and it is superseded by abstract terms such as photons, quarks, waves and particles. But these words do not convey the nature of sunlight as described above. As with all entities without significant physical properties, the inherent identity of sunlight has to be immediately experienced in order to be judiciously known.

While darkness does not have transformational capacity because it is lack of light, yet there remains an apparent tension as light decreases in volume towards darkness. Similarly, sunlight-warmth reduces towards darkness-cold with a suspense reminiscent of that between sunlight and darkness when sunlight is defused and steadily colored as it diminishes towards darkness.

In the very depths of a shadowy corner, the transition of sunlight towards darkness can be recognized through the dark colors of the spectrum. This can be better observed through a magnifying lens. This is not a phenomenon of the lens as it is also visible to the naked eye by its effect upon the surrounding colors.

The decrease of sunlight towards darkness, through minimal color and reflective influence is not as startlingly evident as prismatic colors. Yet, it can still be recognized. All shadows are colored differently. The artist who wishes to paint a cloudy skyscape will enhance the gray with different pigments in order to capture the color nuances. As the corner shadow becomes denser, towards entire darkness, a blue-indigo-violet line is evident particularly if it is contrasted by a faint yellow. Furthermore, the leading edge of an object towards the sun is seen to have a transitional color that is the lighter end of the spectrum. This also is discernible with the naked eye. Further, it is recognized in the way that diffused sunlight illumines the same color pigment in different ways, according to its intensity.

The Haystack paintings of 25 canvasses by Claude Monet, produced at the end of Summer, 1890, and completed in Spring the following year, reveal the effects of sunlight, at different times and seasons, upon the same rural landscape.

The sunlight of late summer is qualitatively, entirely different from the sunlight of Winter and early Spring. The paintings reveal the consequent change in the coloring of the landscape, including the shadows seen as blue against the white snow. The haystack image remains more or less the same but the quality of the sunlight consistently bestows a different illumination effect upon natural colors, which causes a dramatic alteration in appearance.

In terms of qualitative progression, sunlight transforms from its stark condition, moving progressively from the light end of the spectrum through the darker colors, until it becomes insufficiently vigorous to penetrate the darkness. As mentioned above, the leading edge of an object in sunlight is tinged with red-orange-yellow while the trailing edge towards deep shadow is visible as a blue-indigo-violet progression. Thus, the two extremes of the spectrum are recognized as qualitatively different from one another.

The edge towards the sunlight is always illumined by the warm, light colors, and the transition towards darkness always consists of the colder and darker colors. The fact that sunlight can transform into warmth and also be diffused and accordingly illuminate differently is important because it reveals the dimensionality and qualitative significance of its existence. Through experience, we recognize that red, orange and yellow are qualitatively the warmest colors while blue and indigo remain the coldest and the nearest to darkness. As light becomes increasingly diffused and less intense its capacity to warm also decreases. Thus, when sunlight loses the ability to warm, it also colors objects with a cooler palette.

Sunlight may be experienced and qualitatively known under diverse circumstances. The nature of sunlight and how it alters both in color appearance and demeanor, is best described artistically whereby sunlight is recognized, not for apparent physical properties, but for what it in fact is. The range of the quality of luminosity is an infinite palette of interpretation in countless guises of the one colorless, elemental phenomenon.

The poet-scientist, Johann Wolfgang von Goethe, beautifully describes the gradually increasing coloration of a winter landscape towards sunset in the Harz Mountains of northwestern Germany, in the year 1777.

"But as the sun at last was about to set, and its rays, greatly mitigated by the thicker vapors, began to

diffuse a beautiful red color over the whole scene around me the shadow color changed to a green, in lightness to be compared to a sea-green, in beauty to the green of the emerald. The appearance became more and more vivid: one might have imagined oneself in a fairy world, for every object had clothed itself in the two vivid and beautifully harmonizing colors, till at last, the sun went down, the magnificent spectacle was lost in a gray twilight, and by degrees in a clear moon-and-starlight night."

Here Goethe describes the influence of a winter sunset upon the shadowing of a snow covered landscape. The shade is not merely a different depth of gray towards darkness but another color entirely. When sunlight illumines differently through diffusion not only do pigments vary in color but the shadow is also influenced. This implies a more acute relationship between light and darkness than if sunlight and shadow are considered merely at midday. The shadow at bright noon is black and strongly contrasting. When light is differently represented and dramatically diffused by the atmosphere the shadow is not black but colored.

The red sunset that Goethe describes is reflected off the snowy landscape and illumines the shadow cast upon the white snow as green. If one observes the shadow spaces of cracks caused by bright sunlight they are recognized as a black of an equal intensity as the fiery light.

The same cracks viewed in the shadow are orange-yellow. Diffused light no longer produces the stark contrast. The lesser light, by illuminating shadow through coloring, reveals a transition between bright sunlight and black shadow. That transition is recognized through the color effect. When the light has entirely vanished, blackness reigns. Sunset light is of a different quality than noon daylight and illuminates objects weakly as red, influencing the shadowing accordingly. Diffused sunlight illumines differently. The tension between sunlight and darkness is altered in darkness's favor. This is readily apparent through the color quality whereby objects are revealed.

When sunlight is greatly diffused, it is no longer illuminates in the same manner. When sunlight strikes an object, it excites heat according to the degree of the objects' capacity to absorb or reflect. The more diffused the light the less heat it produces. Diffusion reflects and refracts sunlight and reduces its intensity. As sunlight becomes less intense, its capacity to illuminate is reduced from starkness, through color to darkness. Similarly, the quality of its warmth is also reduced.

From the preceding description, we recognize a correspondence between light and heat, but also the correlation between the circumstantial condition of sunlight and that of color temperature.

If one observes the summer sun as it slips behind a range of hills or mountains, it is readily discernible that the shadow side of the ridge is colored differently. At first the shadow color is influenced by the surface color. But, as sunlight diminishes and darkness increasingly holds sway, the shadow cast by the red light of sunset appears blue because waning sunlight produces different shadowing than the powerful sunlight of midday.

Sunlight is essentially incorporeal and, consequently, ideally known through immediate cognition. As with many intangible phenomena, an appreciation of the qualitative significance is most readily achieved through comparison. For example, in terms of recognizing the dynamic nature of the phenomenon of life it is most significantly appreciated when compared to lifelessness. Similarly, the consistency of the archetype and the flexibility in the quality whereby a particular organism is distinguished, is discovered through a comparison between of two variations of the same thing such as the acorns of the black and of white oak trees. They conform to a common archetype, yet they are expressed disparately.

The qualitative identity of sunlight can be ascertained through a comparison between its presence and its absence. To observe these conditions side by side, sunlight may be viewed in relation to the shadow cast by an object. The two situations are observed immediately without intellectual or subjective interference. In other words, if we wish to determine what these conditions of light and darkness are through direct encounter, we can learn of the intrinsic manner of existence directly from the phenomena themselves.

The first thing that we recognize is that there are not two separate conditions but one event. Sunlight and shadow are related through an interplay that is most noticeable when the object is moved or turned. The shadow is not separate from the sunlight.

Further, it is seen that the shadow becomes deeper and more contrasting depending on the intensity of the sunlight. But darkness is passive while sunlight is active. Sunlight can banish the shadow but nevertheless the shadow continues to exist imminently when light is absent, but it cannot encroach upon the light. Furthermore, an object must hinder the sunlight in order for darkness to be apparent. In other words, but for the presence of light, darkness would be pervasive which is an aspect of its own qualitative nature.

Light and darkness are qualitatively different. Light is active while shadow is passive. If there were no object obscuring the sunlight, there would be no shadow transition. If there was no sunlight, there would only be darkness. This dynamic between the two conditions proportionately alters depending on the vividness of the light.

As we stated above, stark sunlight provokes a darker and more strongly contrasting shadow than diffused light. It is through this interaction that the dynamic can be fully appreciated. The more intense the light the deeper the darkness becomes and the clearer the contrast between the two. In very diffused light a shadow is scarcely discernible because darkness is almost imminent. In other words, visually, there is a dynamic between sunlight and shadow but light is substantially more significant because it is active.

The eye will atrophy when a creature remains in total darkness. Creatures that dwell in deep caves or underground lakes lose their sight as well as the actual organ of vision and skin pigmentation. They remain alive because they ingest organisms that are nourished in some capacity, even indirectly by sunlight. But sight and pigment are directly influenced by sunlight itself. Sunlight, therefore, is the formative agency both of the eye and of organic pigmentation, which is color.

It is readily appreciable how sunlight and sun-warmth are both vital media of life. The light quality of the sun and the nature of sun warmth are both of a different character than light and heat produced by artificial means. This has to be experienced in order to be known as it cannot be determined by analysis. But everyone knows the difference for themselves through immediate experience even if the practice of direct cognition remains scientifically suspect. Similarly, the healing and strengthening capacity of sunlight is obvious to traditional medicine and undeniable to sufferers of winter depression.

The skeptical materialist will claim that the qualities described above are merely subjective. But if a living plant is deprived of sunlight it will lose its warm green pigment and yellow, and will soon die even though it has air, warmth, rich soil and abundant water. Plants of a particular, characteristic nature that thrive in shadow typically have a much darker, cold-green coloring because they inhabit the shadow end of the spectrum towards darkness. In complete darkness, of course, they will also perish. The two distinctive natures of sunlight, as illumination and warmth, remain allied and are recognizable as a reciprocity discernible through the color behaviors that exist as a tension between light and darkness.

Sunlight most assuredly incorporates the capacity to quicken and must be recognized as an essential agency of invigoration. Therefore, the capacity to enliven is qualitatively discernible and describes the intrinsic nature of sunlight with the greatest justice.

18. THE NATURE AND MANNER WHEREBY A PHENOMENON IS EXPRESSED
Observations from the Perspective of the Immediate Experience

Quantifiable properties can be readily demonstrated as authentic. The temptation is to disregard the significance of the qualities of things because they remain beyond the reach of physical verification. While they may be physically justified only with difficulty, they are otherwise only subjectively identified as extant. Qualities and intrinsic characteristics can only conclusively determined to be real through direct experience from the perspective of the human, singular distinction of existence.

If something proves to be physically unverifiable, it does not necessarily follow that it does not exist. It could indicate that incorporeal existence is incommensurate with material circumstances. Similarly, a placebo may be instrumental in the restoration of good health. But a placebo does not work. This, demonstrates that the human mind must have extraordinary authority over the wellbeing of the physical body.

Unfortunately, a suspect, scientific methodology has become established that purports to arrive at definitive conclusions through the exhaustive scrutiny and extrapolation of solely measurable and calculable data. Derived from the physical condition of a thing, inevitably corresponding information will be consistently pertinent only in terms of material circumstances.

In other words, the conventional, materialistic practice of philosophical evaluation, requires, ideally, that all phenomena be reduced to calculable properties or arranged in a manner whereby they can be reasoned and logically assessed on the strength of their tangibility. But not all things are solely, physically represented, therefore, and we may not wish to calculate how a thing works. The goal may be to discover what intrinsically a phenomenon actually is.

If an object is solely considered from a physical frame of reference, the intention must be to understand how it functions because thereby, only the mechanics is taken into consideration. We recognize this obsessional perspective as particular dominant in our time. That is, we scrutinize the physics but neglect the essential existence of things. Unfortunately, analytical science now monopolizes the human approach to understanding, overreaching and defining everything in blatant terms. Thus, a phenomenon is described exclusively upon the consideration of its physical properties, and philosophy is similarly circumscribed within those same conditions.

We have a good understanding of how things work from the perspective of the technical sciences, but in our enthusiasm with these successes we have come to believe that the analysis of exclusively insentient properties may be universally applied to define what a phenomenon actually is. Consequently, living, organic forms are degraded to automata and the human being reduced to an amalgamation of the numerous conclusions of the specialized sciences of the inanimate.

The conflict of our time lies between the materialistic perspective and the commonsense recognition of the authenticity of experientially known qualities and the innate circumstances of essentially intangible phenomena. In this sense, we recognize that the materialistic doctrine that dominates popular thinking, is an artificial construct that does not correspond with reality because it is discriminatory.

The self-evident discrepancy between the conclusions of a deductive discipline of understanding concerned solely with physically obvious properties, and the commonplace individual experience of essential value, cannot be simply ignored. Unfortunately, a narrowly slanted view distorts an appropriate relationship towards existence, and is comparable to the madness of tunnel vision.

This antagonistic perspective is further exacerbated by the assumed authority of the specialized sciences as the final arbiter of reality. A pervasive condescension is increasingly apparent, whereby one's own individual experience of reality is rendered moot, in the light of the evidence of dogmatic materialism.

The status and eminence of the scientific perspective, that defines life in terms of its conspicuous properties and workings, are promoted by a mystique of authority established upon the findings of elite specialization. The terminology alone is impossible for the layman to comprehend just as the latinizing of law and religious creed safeguarded the authority of the initiated in earlier centuries.

Every human being has the latent capacity to experience the full dimension of existence, both independently and autonomously. Furthermore, upon the certainty of experientially derived knowledge is established a confidence whereby one is undeceived by the assumed prerogative of an elect professional orthodoxy. Consequently, precepts founded upon abstract-thinking and conclusions derived solely through the intellectual scrutiny of sterile mechanical properties, should not intimidate the individual whose knowledge of reality is acquired through the discipline of immediate cognition.

A purely analytical approach towards understanding, that explores and examines only certain properties, is incomplete, regardless of the weight of accumulated scholarship elaborating those scrutinized aspects. Furthermore, it is insufficient to evaluate life solely through rationale because the intellect is of a construction that is most efficient when it calculates abstractly, and not all phenomena are reducible into quantifiable terms.

While the ideal intellectual discipline is mathematics, the practice of logical argument is a far lesser approach towards substantiation. Mathematics is capable of proving something definitively as long as it can be numerically rendered. But qualities and values are unassimilable through quantification. Therefore, the subordinate tradition of logical argument, however persuasive it may be, is not definitive because argument is flexible and always refutable. That is to say, philosophy is not amenable to appraisal in the manner of accountancy.

Rationale results in only partial understanding because of the inability of the intellect to immediately experience. In other words, the intellect arrives at knowledge only obliquely because it functions indirectly and abstractly. But immediate cognition is capable of directly attaining knowledge concerning the intrinsic existence of things. Therefore, in order to properly understand a phenomenon it needs to be approached experientially and unambiguously.

Immediate experience is a direct encounter with a phenomenon, that establishes a knowledge of the authentic condition. It is an explicit discernment of what the object is in reality. Comparatively, the indirect approach is only superficial because it is, inevitably abstract and circuitous. Conversely, cognition through direct engagement reveals that everything has an essential, qualitative identity and that the intrinsic significance of an object exists intangibly.

The individuality of the human being becomes aware of its own existence through direct cognition. The mind-self is thereby positioned straightforwardly in relationship to the essential of other phenomena, and things are viewed and recognized intrinsically.

While the essential, characteristic nature of a phenomenon cannot be determined through the conventional, materialistic approach and is, consequently, denied existence and excluded from the prevailing, abstract theories concerning life, nevertheless, intrinsic significances are discovered through the agency of immediate cognition. Furthermore, the essential human being thrives upon the direct experience of the substantive nature of things because the unique condition of the individual is of that same essential condition. Thereby, we recognize the limitation of an exclusively materialistic dogma because it defines existence in remote terms.

A definition or explanation founded upon research consisting solely of the mechanical or chemical properties, is fictitious when extended beyond those perspectives to encompass, for example, biological life. If philosophy endeavors to describe life only in those limited terms and thereby reduces reality to an isolated abstract, the conclusions will be inadequate. For example, the reduction of a living entity into its physical components and properties is the only possible approach when analytical reasoning is assumed to be the sole reliable method of human cognition. But that which is neglected and denied is the substantial identity which is assimilable only through direct experience. Consequently, an understanding of life that is established solely upon the apparent, separated properties of an organism is revealed to be insufficiently representational.

The dismemberment of an organism into parts is no longer necessary when the entirety is identified through direct cognition, unless we desire to discover more concerning the workings. But with respect to the intrinsic identity of things, analytical examination is an indirect approach that is always insufficient because it cannot determine the distinction of the entirety. Accordingly, while a creature may be classified and acknowledged by its physical properties, yet remains unidentified in relation to its particular condition of existence because it is still descriptively nameless.

In other words, in order to grasp the mechanics or chemistry of a phenomenon and re-apply those laws through human invention, the conventional, scientific methodology must obviously be retained. However, immediately experienced knowledge of the actual identity of an object will temper investigation and restrain the application of partial knowledge as a philosophical basis of understanding existence.

The barrier to complete knowledge is ignorance of the value of direct cognition and a consequent failure to recognize the significance of qualitative distinctions beyond the obvious, physical appearances. It is founded upon the assumption that a greater capacity of knowledge is attainable through reasoning than the intellect is able to supply. The limited scope of deductive logic is overlooked because direct cognition is a virtually unknown ability, dismissed as merely subjective assessment.

Consequently, if direct cognition is considered subjective, the qualitative significance of circumstances is entirely discarded as unprovable and the physical state is subsequently overemphasized. Hence, the failure to explore immediate cognition immediately and objectively for oneself from the perspective of the human, intrinsic identity. If these issues are ignored then the researcher is condemned to a slanted, distorted and disingenuous world-view.

It is important to directly experience qualitative realities in order to ascertain the intrinsic condition of a phenomenon and to discover the authentic distinction of the object that one is dealing with. Immediate knowledge of the inherent identity is both essential and pivotal to existential knowledge. If one knows what a thing essentially is, a far more significant understanding becomes available than the statistical account of the physical properties.

The description of an essential-nature is bound to be figurative and metaphorical because it relates to intangible values and non-material characteristics. The language of art is the way in which incorporeal qualities are best described. An example of this is the depiction of the mineral granite by the German poet-scientist, Goethe. (Johann Wolfgang von Goethe 1749 – 1832, *On Granite*).

Nowhere in his description is there a mention of chemical formulae or the Mohs scale of mineral hardness, or atomic structure. Yet, the artistic lucidity of his representation thoroughly identifies the essential and actual identity of the mineral

Similarly, the English poet and visual artist, William Blake (1757 – 1827) used his considerable skill as a painter to portray the essential identity of a flea. The *Ghost of a Flea* includes no information regarding taxonomic rank, protein composition, the mechanics of the jump or the insect's metamorphic cycle. Yet, it entirely describes the character-nature, articulated through the art-language of painting.

When the description of a phenomenon is limited to its sterile, physical properties, its authentic identity remains overlooked. However, the shortcomings of purely material evaluation are revealed through a comparison between the conclusions of an abstract, cerebral discipline and knowledge through direct encounter. Thereby the immediate experience of the essential nature reveals the real identity of a phenomenon. Knowledge, achieved through immediate experience, elevates cognition from an examination of superficial properties to the profound discernment of essential identities.

Ghost of a Flea – William Blake

19. THE HUMAN CAPACITY OF DIRECT COGNITION
Human, Conscious Individuality

Direct cognition is a practice whereby the human, particular ipseity straightforwardly and unambiguously meets the essential significance of a phenomenon of interest. Usually, we rely on established preconceptions whereby we seek to match the object judiciously with established ideas and memories in order to discover a similarity, but in terms of immediate engagement all preconceptions must be inhibited.

The conventional, circuitous way of assessing something is vulnerable to distortion, misrepresentation and error because it occurs tangentially. However, direct cognition requires that conceptual association be set aside in order that the phenomenon may be encountered afresh upon its own, original merits. That is to say, the purpose of immediate engagement is to discover the intrinsic relevance of something for what it in fact is and not what we feel or reason it to be.

Consequently, through direct experience, the object is met without the diffusion of associative assessment or feeling evaluation, but it is apprehended directly by the essential, human distinction. Phenomena are experienced and straightforwardly known instead of being interpreted, and thereby the application of the human faculty of direct cognition leads to autonomous knowledge. In this sense, we discover the definitive nature of the existence of something and engage essential conditions in present timing.

In order to navigate the phenomenal world with a significant autonomy of cognition, it requires the recognition of things as they are and not merely as we conceive them to be. Consequently, a sole consideration of physical properties only reveals a distorted and exclusively materialistic perspective. Thereby, we recognize the damage done by an intrusive, materially prejudiced philosophy against understanding existence as it really is. Similarly, faith in a religious dogma or esoteric perspective are indirect approaches to knowledge and subject to distortion and misinterpretation unless directly authenticated through immediate cognition. Indeed, every indirect conceptual approach removed from actual experience is inevitably abstract, in contrast with the straightforward engagement of an actual event.

The autonomous authority of the human being lies within the intrinsic, individual significance of a person. Accordingly, from the perspective of the human, essential singularity of existence, we can directly determine what something is because the ipseity is of the same unequivocal nature as the essential identity of things. In other words, the human, conscious individuality comes to know itself through experiential self-recognition, thereupon it directly discerns the same intrinsic significance of all other things.

While immediate cognition may at first seem to be a mystical excess, in fact it is conventional cognition that is remote. Straightforwardly ascertained knowledge, offers first-hand information concerning the intrinsic significance of things that, unlike subjective appraisal, can be corroborated as authentic through the similarly immediate experience of another person. Thereupon, a situation is not only individually and separately discerned but anyone can engage circumstances directly and impartially for themselves and discover the essential, characteristic nature of phenomena. This is because there is not a profusion of possible distinctions but only one actual identity that exists not in the interpretation but inherently as the intrinsic significance of the thing itself.

The dogma of the materialist insists upon a definition of the human self that is solely corporeal. Apparently, the self is established within the material biology of the human being and the human individuality is attributed merely to neurological singularity. The materialist must work diligently to maintain this device because it contradicts direct experience that justifies intangible human significance. Therefore, qualitative evidence must be dismissed from assessment otherwise the entire premise of physical exclusivity is threatened. Thereby, we recognize that materialistic, Western philosophy is a dogma like any other, the leading premises of which must be constantly reinforced and reiterated because abstractly and artificially contrived, they contradict reality.

Theories of this disposition abound because speculative evaluation calculates and determines an interpretation of existence based upon exclusively, physical data. It is imagined that a premise established upon physical evidence is exclusively authentic. It does not occur to the materialist that the corporeal perspective may be too narrow.

Unfortunately, these abstract systems remain compelling because constructs that are logically followed seem true if we understand the rationale. They appear more palatable than scarcely recognized direct knowledge because being reasoned, they look soundly structured. Indeed, in the face of rationale, immediate experience is denied validity because it is not physically represented. In other words, we know where the brain is, but the physically elusive ipseity remains dissociative. Consequently, materialistically established philosophy disdains the idea of essential knowledge and intangible value discerned through immediate experience. The intellect works only indirectly and abstractly and, consequently, it is an inadequate practice when the goal is irrefutable knowledge.

Understanding through rationale, sentimental conviction and the vagaries of mysticism all pale beside direct cognition. They lack the capacity to know reality at first hand and, consequently, they are incapable of discovering the human, conscious individuality. Ironically, open the practice of immediate cognition the observer inevitably discovers the essential self because the intrusive faculties are of necessity inhibited. However, through indirect evaluation, definitive knowledge attained through immediate experience remains inaccessible.

The researcher must pay careful attention to the reality of incorporeal significances and notice those things during everyday life that are authentic yet, remain intangible. This will begin to loosen the restricted grip that materialism has imposed.

Thereafter, the practice of immediate experience can reveal the authenticity of the individual self and direct cognition becomes possible to the degree that the essential, human singularity is established as the sovereign authority of our constitution. Furthermore, phenomena become recognized for their intrinsic significance when the essential identity of the human being asserts an unrestricted, cognitive prerogative.

As the effort is made to quiet the intellect and focus and attention are established from the perspective of the essential, human self, intrinsic conditions through direct encounter becomes recognizable as a vastly more significant than the banal appearance.

20. THE IMMEDIATE EXPERIENCE OF REALITY With Reference to the Works of Rene Descartes

Descartes presented a flawed structure of cognition that, while it comprehensively addressed all aspects of human perception, it relied primarily on abstract reasoning supported by religious conviction. Unfortunately, although exhaustively contemplated, it embodied a distortion and misrepresentation because Descartes lacked sufficient knowledge and familiarity with the inherent, human capacity of immediate cognition. He failed to establish a connection between the direct, experiential knowledge that he had achieved concerning his own incorporeal significance and the similarly essential dimension of external phenomena.

If the experiential recognition of his own intrinsic existence, had been extended to encompass other phenomena, it would have revealed to Descartes the presence of an extant, intangible volume of crucial significance that is inherent to all things. Thereby, he would have established an authentic and definitive cognitional approach. Instead, he endeavored to justify the knowledge of his own experientially discovered reality as if he had discerned it, not immediately, but primarily through abstract rationale.

The recognition and identification of the self as the sovereign identity of the human being is not a simple task because of the compelling materially established evidence to the contrary. It requires diligent application but therein lies its merit. If it were effortless, we could not possibly achieve autonomy because our own endeavor is as essential to our awakening, as the struggle of a child learning to stand.

It is only through concerted effort that we progress from a materially circumscribed view of existence and cognitively emancipate ourselves, becoming alert to the permanency of things, which is their authentic condition.

Descartes explored the possibility of a methodology of reason that would provide a structure by means of which the real from the unreal might be differentiated. He confused this research by equating real and unreal with true and false. Failure to establish a distinction between the two, obscured the dissimilarity between abstract reasoning and experiential knowledge. In other words, rationale may reveal truth but only direct cognition by the mind-self can achieve experiential knowledge of what is real.

Descartes assumed that the abstract calculation that determine the correct and the incorrect was a compatible approach towards the discovery of reality. He failed to recognize that they represent incommensurate conditions. That is to say, the differentiation between truth and falsehood is determined through logical calculation, but reality is a state of existence that must be engaged in order to be known. Furthermore, in essence, there is no such thing in reality as unreality, except from the perspective of madness.

Thereby, solipsism became a cognitive obstruction, whereas knowledge of the human, intrinsic ipseity should have offered an essential point of view upon the strength of which substantive reality could have been discerned. This oversight obscured the possibility of an experiential discovery of the full dimension of existence by the same means whereby he had first discovered his own significance through immediate engagement.

      The basis of Descartes's philosophy rested upon the experiential recognition of the reality of his own being as the ultimate standard of certainty. The flaw lay in the application of incommensurate approaches towards incompatible inquiries. He coupled the authentication of experience to mathematical justification because he equated a successful theorem with proof of reality. Descartes wanted to apply mathematical exactitude as a means to determine the authenticity of philosophical premises. In other words, he recognized something impeccable and irrefutable in mathematics and determined to calculate existence as if being were numerically reducible. However, while a demonstrated proof has an oblique aesthetic similarity to an experience of essential existence, nevertheless, the two differ qualitatively. The one is the consequence of deliberation ideally applicable to quantities, while the other is a non-quantifiable state or condition that must be experienced in order to be justified.

      Descartes applied reasoning to justify the achievement of an experiential knowledge of the reality of his own being. Furthermore, the existence of his own essential self was qualified through the recognition of his thinking activity instead of his capacity to observe. Consequently, Descartes attributed direct knowledge of the essential self to his capacity of reason and overlooked that direct cognition and not the intellect had revealed the reality of his intrinsic existence. While the existence of the intrinsic self can be semantically argued, it must be immediately experienced in order to be definitively known. Ironically, the abstract reasoning Descartes applied as a justification for his own essential reality might just as easily have been counter-argued to disprove his own existence.

The qualitative, intangible significances that are experienced directly through immediate cognition, reveal the essential condition of the existence of an object. The human essence is of that same caliber, and that is how we are able to experientially discover the intrinsic nature of other phenomena.

The indirect, intellectual approach considers qualitative value with suspicion because intangible conditions cannot be physically verified. From a materialistic point of view, it is assumed that they are merely subjective experiences, undependable and elusive. Consequently, if value cannot be reduced into quantifiable terms, the significance of qualitative distinction is dismissed from serious appraisal, as philosophically irrelevant. This occurs because the intellect cannot rationalize incorporeal significances if they are only revealed by immediate experience and remain inaccessible through physical means. Nevertheless, the foundational premise of Descartes's philosophy is established upon the recognition of the reality of his own existence, and this discovery was not achieved through reason but through experiential engagement.

Reasoning functions abstractly from the event and, consequently, deals most effectively with mathematical aggregates and the management of logical sequences. It is not successfully extended to demonstrate qualitative value and essential existences because they are incongruous by virtue of their intangibility. The truth of the existence of the being of Descartes cannot be justified by the intellect. To know of his own identity, Descartes would have had to experience it directly.

Furthermore, the statement *I think, therefore I am,* is of doubtful validity. While thinking is readily justifiable as a viable human activity, *being* is only known through experience. The capacity to reason does not necessarily demonstrate the existence of human identity but the self-awareness of the observer does. That is to say, thinking of itself does not demonstrate the existence of being but only that of a function. But the observer, observing the respective action of the self while observing, experientially reveals the existence of the unique self.

Differently expressed, the implication is that the existence of a thinker is proven because of the activity of thought. But thinking only implies being through implication. However, immediate cognition does not require inference because it engages directly. That is to say, the recognition of the thinker as an intransient entity requires justification through direct experience. But while the existence of the authentic, human identity necessarily precedes every activity including thinking as an act of personal volition, the *I am* of Descartes is not justified because he can think but exists inviolately in its own right. It is not thinking that demonstrates and qualifies the reality of the intrinsic, human being, but it is the individuality itself experiencing its own intrinsic existence.

The intellect is a human, corporeal faculty. It is a

function without personal identity. The intellect cannot recognize itself because it does not possess intrinsic, individual status and self-recognition mandates the existence of an entity, not merely a function. Needless to say, the *I am* of Descartes is an extant entity with a self that can be experientially discerned and does not require rationalization in order to demonstrate its existence.

Frequently, the spontaneous occurrence of knowledge is confusingly described as both insight and intuition. Both terms fail to describe the event with adequate justice. In the modern vernacular, intuition is attributed to something capricious and mysterious while the materialistic view of insight is interpreted as an exclusively neural activity, which is equally unhelpful.

Through direct, experiential cognition by the singular distinction of the human being, immediate knowledge is apparent as an inherent condition. This is because the essential, human singularity and the intrinsic status of the phenomenon reside within the same intangible condition of existence.

After establishing a dissonant correspondence between reason and experience, Descartes had hoped to establish a methodology towards cognitive autonomy founded upon reason alone. He endeavored to elevate the reasoning, abstract mind to the station of the primary and exclusive means of human cognition. He wanted the cognitional practice to be methodically structured, resembling immaculate mathematical proof and, further, established as the final arbiter of reality. Thereby he incorrectly attributed qualitative knowledge to reasoning when in fact essential significances could only have been immediately ascertained.

Applying abstract reasoning to all things in order to achieve certainty, Descartes, reduced organic life into quantitative terms. Hence, his elaborate depiction of organisms as mechanical processes. In other words, he recognized the mechanisms at work in nature and extrapolated a definition of existence upon those exclusive conditions.

In order to achieve a definitive conclusion, satisfactory to Descartes, this abstracted data was necessarily mathematical and mechanical by nature because it must be of a structure that can be reasoned. Thus, living, growing and metamorphosing organic life-forms are represented as a lifeless automaton that operate through the physical expansion and contraction of fluids. Descartes discounts the qualitative and applies an enormously disproportionate emphasis upon the mechanically identifiable properties, establishing an intellectual fiction in the place of reality.

The modern, analytical approach to biology similarly reduces living organic-forms to their mechanical, and consequently, abstractly manageable essentials. This is inevitable as sequential logic deals ideally with quantities and cannot readily assimilate incorporeal values.

If a summation of life is to be simplified and reduced in accordance with a particular emphasis such as the pure physical, there is little the investigator can do with elusive, essential values. Yet, while an organic form can be imagined as if it were a machine, mechanics does not define a living entity it merely isolates the laws that circumscribe its workings. If mechanical activities are recognized at work in living creatures it does not follow that an animal or plant exists solely as a mechanism. In other words, the significance of a phenomenon is independent of its chemical, physical or electrical systems because mechanisms alone fail to describe the intrinsic distinction of the entire expression of the existence of something. Indeed, processes are deceptive if we assume that function is synonymous with identity.

At work in reality, is an indivisible integrity of wholeness wherein no aspect of a phenomenon may be discarded without the disintegration of the value of the entirety. Yet, the entirety and its identity are discounted when the form is dismembered, analyzed and defined in separate physical terms. It is unknown, for example, what life itself is, but rather than elevate this significant phenomenon to foremost prominence in scientific inquiry, it is conveniently overlooked, along with much that is critical to understanding an actual living, growing and reproducing organic entirety.

Descartes's descriptions of the reciprocal interplay between the soul and the biochemical bodily functions are both simplistic and quaint to modern scholarship. What they have in common with contemporary biology, however, is that both describe living phenomena in the same physical manner, exclusively of the significance of the identity of the organism. Consequently, incorporeal realities such as the human ipseity and also, the phenomenon of life itself, remain cognitively elusive without immediate, experiential apprehension. As we have already stated, intangible, intrinsic distinction cannot be recognized and known through deductive process, particularly if our view is concerned solely with the physical carapace.

In other words, while information concerning the physical properties of a phenomenon can be readily assessed, qualities are only explored and known for their intrinsic identity through immediate experience. Consequently, If understanding is founded solely upon materialistically justified properties and mechanical cause-and-effect, then the intrinsic identity will remain forever elusive. The outcome of an excessively physical emphasis will consist merely of an amalgamation of the superficially evident properties, and a very distorted impression of reality will result. Those ignored qualitative values, incompatible and incomprehensible to abstract reasoning because they are intangible and cannot be physically authenticated, can be recognized only through an immediate engagement of the phenomenon. Unlike subjective experience, they are justified because the intrinsic identity of the human being is ultimately essential and inevitably it encounters the substantive significance of phenomena with appropriate directness.

In other words, like Descartes, we discover the authenticity of our own, singular existence through immediate cognitional engagement. Henceforth, from the perspective of our own singularly extant entity, we experientially engage phenomena and discover their intrinsic nature. That is, we experience our own sovereign individuality and recognize the same essential significance that similarly comprise other phenomena.

The prevalent mechanical model of existence that has become the readily amenable explanation of life is the direct result of the assumption that only the physically recognizable properties of a phenomenon are real. Nevertheless, everyone, of course, knows the existence of intangible qualities and significances through day to day experience. But we cannot demonstrate their existence in physically acceptable terms because they remain intangible. Consequently, we go along with an absurdly narrow philosophy that defies commonsense, and we watch as a warped perspective increasingly diminishes human optimism and meaningful pursuit.

Descartes suffered from the same quandary. He failed to apply the means whereby he recognized his own authenticity as a significant practice of cognition. Therefore, he could never arrive at a definitive comprehension of intrinsic existence but tried to compress the direct experience of the intrinsic self into mechanistic parameters. He could not discern the authentic, intangible constitution of existence because he did not realize the significance of the requisite perspective of the essential ipseity. Consequently, he remained caught in this dilemma trying to interpret phenomena through rationale alone when only immediate experience could reveal the intrinsic importance of things.

Descartes experienced his intrinsic selfhood immediately through direct cognition. He could not do so in any other way because the authentic identity of the human being is incorporeal and cannot be demonstrated as existent by any means that relies only upon material assessment. Because the self exists in a manner physically unidentifiable and unmanageable through intellectual calculation, Descartes was compelled to qualify his experience through contrived, abstract reasoning. Therefore, as stated earlier, convinced of the infallibility of mathematical processes he equated a demonstrated mathematical proof with reality, thereby confusing the true and false of mathematics with the real or non-existence of experience. He denied the intrinsic authenticity of the qualitative attributes of phenomena because they are unquantifiable and irreducible, and consequently unamenable to strict calculation. In consequence, the subsequent mechanical interpretation of existence was a too narrow view that was clearly fictional when applied as an existential interpretation of the entirety.

The contradiction of Descartes's approach lies in the self-recognition of his intransient existence through immediate experience whereby the self discovers its own authenticity, and his antithetical denial of immediate cognition when it came to the apprehension of other phenomena. He saw all other things superficially and defined them on the basis of their mechanical functions. In this sense, he blocked the discovery of essential, elemental conditions that are the significance of all physical manifestation because he did not extend the recognition of his own intrinsic existence beyond himself and the mystical experience of God. If he done so, he would have discovered universal essentiality from the perspective of the individual, imperative ipseity that epitomized self existence.

The implication of the mechanical devaluation of physical phenomena is the excruciating analysis of material circumstances and the positioning of the peripheral view as if it were the entirety of existence. Thereby, the shallow perspective has been compounded and extrapolated with increasing enthusiasm by lesser minds ever since, with the consequence of the accepted establishment of a dreary and meaningless world-view.

Descartes considered sense information fallible. Abstractly, he argued that the senses were incapable of providing consistently viable information. This was a conjecture entirely isolated from direct experience. It was a construct founded upon the belief that the senses were somehow independent channels of information. This is a direct extension of Descartes's mechanical world-view in which the parts of an organization have a separate existence while the entirety is defined merely as an amalgamation. He did not recognize entireties but thought only in terms of the combination of separate parts.

Unable to discover the intrinsic entirety that qualitatively distinguishes a phenomenon, he overlooked the dynamic elasticity of the inquiring human mind that constantly sifts and evaluates intelligence. He considered the mind as at the mercy of fallible, sense information while in fact the human being uses and directs the thoroughly integrated senses, at will. The senses are an extension of human cognition but Descartes granted them autonomous significance. Thus, he reduced the energetic mind to the status of passive and bewildered unfortunate, while abstractly he determined that the unreliable senses presented suspect and questionable information. The absurd yet, logical conclusion to this abstract fabrication was that material phenomena may not even exist.

Descartes managed to separate his own singular significance that he had initially discovered through immediate experience, from the rest of existence. Thereby, the discovery of the human ipseity became less an essential priority of view and the portal of existential knowledge, but unrealistically assumed an isolated, egoistic position that could potentially dominate the human heart.

For this reason a natural euphoria originating from the recognition of human, individual uniqueness must be tempered by the experiential knowledge of the equivalent distinction of everyone else, and of the intrinsic manner of the existence of phenomena. That is to say, the human individuality has the capacity of direct cognitional engagement and thereby wields the full resources of the human entirety towards an object of interest. Yet, while abstractly, the human being may be divided into parts, in practice it must always function within the context the entirety, including respect and goodwill towards the similarly unique distinction of everyone else.

The irony remains, that Descartes had already discovered and identified the reality of the unique and singular self through immediate experience. If he practiced the same capacity of direct cognition farther beyond self-recognition, he would have discovered the distinction between experiential engagement and abstract, intellectual evaluation. Thereby he would have found no need to pursue a mechanistic interpretation of existence. Obviously, things operate physically but their existence is not determined solely upon the basis of mechanical functionality.

In other words, the human, unique distinction is intrinsic and incorporeal wherein lies the capacity of essential discernment. Through immediate engagement the unique ipseity experiences the crucial significance of things and not merely the superficial. But for Descartes that glimpse of self-certainty provoked a conflict between abstract rationale and directly ascertained knowledge. Unfortunately, in the seventeenth century probably no one recognized the more profound significance and greater application of immediate cognition, in a conscious manner. If he had directed the attention of the mind-self beyond the recognition of its own authenticity and observed outwardly from that selfsame perspective, he would have discovered the full volume of essential existence inherent within the phenomenal world.

Descartes was searching for a practice that would reveal infallible truth. Consequently, he stretched and extended mathematics beyond its justified scope as if logic were similarly conclusive. Unfamiliar with the inherent accessibility of objective knowledge through immediate experience by the incorporeal self, he selected abstract calculation in its place in order to comprehend human and phenomenal existence. Thereby, he approached life in the dualistic terms of the intrinsic human soul and an alien, sensational world. This fractured world-view reduced existence to an unrealistic arrangement wherein the self was opposite to everything else. Thereby, immediate knowledge of intrinsic being was obscured.

In terms of immediate cognition, the possibility of self-deception is often used to disparage the practice, whereupon materialism is presented as a more reliable approach to understanding as if it were a viable option. However, the exercise of direct engagement by the human conscious individuality requires a significance of honesty and discipline so that knowledge is not confused with preconception, prejudice, imagination or sentiment.

That discipline is at least as stringent as Descartes's methodology of unprejudiced, alert and clear reasoning. Further, unlike a conviction based upon feeling or imagination, authentic knowledge is corroborative. It deals with the real identity of things, and consequently, a person is not required to believe but to explore for oneself and compare.

In order to engage the essential existence of phenomena with the same empirical restraint with which reason it applied to evaluate material conditions, the capacity of direct cognition must be applied in a thoroughly disciplined and scrupulous manner. Descartes had this ability, but he failed to recognize immediate cognition and subsequent, conclusive knowledge as a fundamental propensity of the self. He did not realize that the recognition of the authenticity of his own self was evidence of the latent human capacity of direct cognition, the application of which would have led to an autonomy of understanding far in advance of reason. It would have revealed phenomena in their immediate, extant condition.

It is indicative of Descartes's integrity to the demands of his methodology that he denied verifiable reality to any properties other than figure, magnitude and motion. Unfortunately, he thereby reduced his definition and description of the world to fit entirely within those mechanistic and artificially, reduced terms. However, the dismissal of intangible evidence betrayed the cause of rationale that he otherwise championed. That is to say, the exclusion of the essential evidence of quality and value is inherently illogical because the human being knows the authenticity of intangible significances through ordinary experience tempered by commonsense.

Continuing forward from the time of Descartes, the materialistic myopia of Western philosophy continues to renounce essential value, and the qualitative dimension of phenomena, including elemental identity and inherent distinction, are summarily discounted.

What Descartes and the modern materialist seek to achieve is world-view consisting solely of properties that can be identified through measurement and verified through calculation and logical, sequential reasoning. Only a thinker who is voluntarily blind to the intangible dimension of existence can sustain such a distorted perspective. Consequently, although attributed to reason because of its exclusive one-sidedness, materialism can only be regarded as an abstract contrivance.

Furthermore, describing biology unequivocally in terms of its physical properties and mechanical functions, with considerable assistance from the imagination, Descartes arrived at a clever but extraordinarily simplistic justification. This is the inevitable consequence of thinking exclusively in the abstract. He compared and identified the movements of a manufactured contrivance that bear no resemblance to the reality of the human body beyond the vague use of a common terminology of description. Similarly, although less simplistically and, with the weight of an intimidating orthodoxy, modern science assumes a monopoly of opinion as to what constitutes reality founded exclusively upon materialistic, mechanical concepts.

Descartes conceded to the difficulty of determining the particular identity of a phenomenon. Instead, he suggested that a problem be reduced into smaller aspects through analysis and then reconsidered in a piece-meal fashion. Reductionism is the way of mathematics and the manner in which reason is able to manage a cognitive task otherwise beyond its scope. This was an unavoidable strategy but it occasioned the loss of the phenomenal entirety whereby the intrinsic and characteristic nature of something may become otherwise known. Unfortunately, the intrinsic condition of the existence of something is unrecognizable through reductionism.

Descartes allocated to rationale the final arbitration of truth. Where he inadvertently confused true and false as mathematical values, with real and nonexistence as experiential conditions, he found himself unable to successfully demonstrate an argument. Being a man of considerable integrity, he admitted defeat and allocated the solution exclusively to the capacity of Deity, and beyond the ability of human comprehension.

But his conclusion was incorrect because all things are recognizable for their intrinsic condition of existence through the innate, human capacity of direct cognition. There are only limits on the reach of deduction.

Descartes's quandary rested upon the several, essential confusions. As we stated earlier, the mathematical values of true or false are incommensurate with the determination of reality. Furthermore, incorporeal, intrinsic significance extends to all phenomena and is distinguishable through immediate cognition, while reason is only definitive in the management of mathematically calculable quotas. Consequently, logic, remote from the exactitude of mathematics, is uncertain because abstract thinking always functions obliquely from an actual event.

Descartes's abstract world-view consisted almost entirely of quantifiable components that can be mathematically managed. That is, data that can be reduced to figure, dimension and motion. Descartes recognized that the intellect functioned most accurately and efficiently when occupied with mathematics. He endeavored to establish a logical approach resembling the same, through sequential, progressive deduction.

But when he applied the calculation to qualitative values he found the need to draw upon capacities of cognition that did not exist within his methodology. He attributed his conclusions vaguely to: *reasonable and clear findings; common sense;* or *beyond human knowledge and exclusive to the realm of Deity.* By this admission he revealed the parameters and shortcomings of abstract intellectualism.

The intangible value of a phenomenon is unrecognizable except through direct experience. Experientially achieved knowledge is necessarily subjective but it is tempered through the discipline and directness of the approach consequently subjectively derived knowledge is not without value. Even though its appraisal is inconsistent, a subjectively identified phenomenon may still exist. However, conclusive evidence concerning the intangible distinction and value of a phenomenon, is achievable when the intrinsic existence of the human being that Descartes discovered, is established as the sovereign perspective. That is to reiterate, the human, singular distinction of existence can directly engage phenomena and discover the intrinsic condition of their existence.

Descartes failed to recognize immediate

experience as a natural, cognitive capacity for the assimilation of knowledge even though he must have used it himself in order to identify the reality of the human *I am*. The essential identity of the human being can only be recognized experientially because it is incorporeal. Through reason and deduction it is unapproachable in any definitive way. Preoccupied with his intellectual ability, Descartes denied significance to the qualitative dimension of natural phenomena and elevated the faculty of thinking as if it were commensurate with existence. When his commonsense held sway he attributed the qualitative a begrudged reality but soon descended once again to the opinion that what could not be measured nor calculated was therefore, most probably illusory as it could not be objectively verified. However, intangible significances are incommensurate with the material standards that permit absolute representation, and cannot be physically verified as extant.

However, through immediate experience we endeavor to determine what a phenomenon is in its own right without distorting it through definition and argument. From Descartes we learn that abstract intellectualism functions best when manipulating mathematically arranged symbols that are purely quantitative and conceptual. However, numerical symbolism describes tangible attributes only to the degree that they can be quantified. That is, mathematics presents information regarding certain aspects but it is otherwise a poor substitute for knowledge of the actual phenomenon because measurable properties alone do cannot represent the entirety of any physical situation.

The cognitive practice necessary in order to

know the intrinsic significance of a phenomenon is immediate experience through the aegis of the human singular distinction. The experience of direct encounter and the concurrent, existential knowledge that becomes evident, reveals the same significance in the contemplated phenomenon as that which constitutes the essential human ipseity because both are incorporeally extant.

We recognize through immediate experience and the knowledge that arises through the human conscious individuality, two things that are absolutely real. The first is the incorporeal self of Descartes that he described as *I am*. The second is the intrinsic identity of phenomenal reality. This is more than merely the material appearance, it is the inherent epitome of the phenomenon whose essential condition rests upon its characteristic distinction.

The foundation of Descartes's perspective is his desire to establish a methodology whereby all things might be verified by infallible reason so that their veracity might be justified beyond doubt. He wished to understand existence with certainty. Unfortunately, the ideal language of the intellect is mathematical in nature. But the entirety of existence is not mathematically reducible. In other words, a point may be argued logically along the lines of mathematics and as honestly as possible, but the outcome is not proof, it is dialectic. Restricting the definition of a phenomenon to data that is measurable and calculable, establishes a world-view solely constructed upon those obvious properties.

Recognizing this as Descartes's practice, his conclusions are consequently only justified from a restricted and limited perspective. While intellectually rationalized, they remain ultimately unreal. This is the consequence of an excessively abstract consideration of existence untempered by direct experience.

Modern materialism has adopted Descartes's philosophy only in part. Contained within his approach were essentials that made it at least structurally, complete. The additional and conventionally discarded aspects include Deity, commonsense and intuition. Descartes himself, wrestled with all three, eventually resolving the discrepancies to his satisfaction and establishing a workable structure. Materialistic, Western philosophy has retained abstract reasoning concerning the physical appearance alone as the primary means of cognition. That is why the modern perspective towards existence is strongly slanted towards superficial appearances.

To establish a similarly concise construct, without reintroducing Descartes's properties of Deity, commonsense and intuition, we would have to replace them with capacities that resolve the shortcomings of the intellect but do not rely upon belief or faith to do so. We need a practice of cognition that recognizes the reality of intangible essentiality that are otherwise maligned by the materialistic mentality. Descartes argued that mathematics and the laws of physics were eternal yet found them insufficiently flexible and had to include other less than certain practices to establish an authentic methodology that embraced all human experience.

The neglected, cognitive practice that provides comprehensive knowledge concerning the essential existence of phenomena, is immediate experience.

However, prerequisite to knowledge through the aegis of the human, conscious individuality, is the suspension of intellectual preoccupation and subjective perception, in order that things may be directly experienced and their authentic condition, subsequently recognized.

Descartes did not know how to refine the manner in which he achieved an immediate, experiential knowledge of his own self, in order that it might, as a viable cognitive perspective, qualify reason and anchor the imagination through a direct apprehension of the real and actual.

Neither did he explore how immediately ascertained knowledge reveals significances in the world of Nature that are superficially and abstractly unfathomable. Consequently, his abstract view established a perspective isolated and remote from reality and, without direct cognition, he had to introduce solutions, such as Deity and commonsense, to compensate for his inability to intellectually fathom intangibles. Finding the qualitative beyond the reach of the intellect, he either abandoned it as God's exclusive prerogative or denied its existence altogether.

Experiential knowledge of the condition of reality through the direct encounter of the human, singular distinction, tempers both abstract imagination and subjective perception. This is because, familiarity with the extant condition of things is of ultimate consequence and serves as a benchmark of reality.

Abstract imagination concerning the physical appearance of phenomena persists in elaborating concepts founded upon partial data. Consequently, imaginative hypotheses and theoretical models increasingly become accepted and established as a substitute reality by both orthodox and popular accord. Thereby, intellectualism constructs a contrived, abstract world-view by grafting a theoretical structure upon existence and requiring reality to comply.

This predictable fabrication is the direct result of the unrecognized shortcomings of materialistic, Western philosophy. It is compounded by a surrender to the monopolistic authority of scholarship and technological expertise. If the orthodox view neglects to admit the shortcomings of its methodology and fails to concede that much that is proclaimed as real is in actuality, abstract hypotheses, then the individual, through commonsense, will consider the matter incomplete and strive for understanding by other means. If the orthodoxy of the academic community presents unproven theory, agreed as fact by consensus, as sufficient validation, then their assertions of veracity are likewise reduced to the status of considered opinion and mere belief and we will correctly consider their work a misrepresentation of reality.

A world definition through Descartes's methodology, void of the imperative of qualitative significance, results in the isolation of essentials as an illusive and mystical factor of minor significance compared to quantitatively reducible, physical properties. Yet, that which cannot be reasoned can be known through immediate experience. That is to say, the reality of incorporeal essentials can be individually justified, mutually corroborated and profoundly known through direct knowledge.

Phenomena, encountered through the human,

singular distinction of existence, and the condition of reality directly experienced through the agency of the individual entity, are indeed qualitatively different from the constructs of abstract reason. Thereby, the direct experience of the condition of actuality reveals knowledge of vastly more profound significance.

As incommensurate as truth with reality, is the juxtaposition between that which is quantifiable with that of qualitative significance. Through the summary dismissal from prevailing Western philosophy, of the meaningfulness of intangible merit, we can only assume that the cognitive practices that apply to the physical are imagined to be similarly pertinent to the intangible. It is upon the strength of the exclusive manner whereby we evaluate the physical that the intangible significance of phenomena is maligned.

While Descartes doubted the reliability of sense-information unless it could be independently measured, the neglected qualitative aspects of phenomena, discarded by such a practice, were the very ones that might have revealed the essential reality of the object. Descartes argued away reality through logic. Yet, immediate experience always confronts existence face-to-face and thereby we determine intrinsically what a thing is. Direct cognition reveals philosophical constructs as moot to the degree that they are limited within merely quantitative parameters.

As the authenticity of direct cognition is increasingly recognized as a valid and significant experience of knowledge concerning essential identities and intangible values, it distances itself from a misidentification with superstition and its dubious historical reputation, as well as from modern, dilettante mysticism.

Direct cognition requires exploration and practice by the modern mind schooled in the integrity of disciplined procedure and systematic exploration. While qualities and values cannot be directly evaluated through the intellect, the pragmatism and restraint of ordered thinking are of immense value. Vague, capricious experiences and their subsequent misinterpretation as authoritative knowledge, are diminished through an integrity of approach that demands and insists upon the authentic.

The obvious difficulty with an evaluation of qualities is that they cannot be assessed through physical means and must be experienced. Therefore, the approach must be of a different nature. To deny the qualitative attributes of a phenomenon, because they are incomprehensible through reason, is paramount to madness because we experience them all the time. However, a tentative exploration through the practice of immediate, experiential engagement, restraining the intrusion of the busy intellect and the host of established preconceptions that eagerly intrude themselves in place of a direct recognition, will reveal a valid cognitive approach. Through the perspective of the human, individual entity, upon diligent investigation, it will be discovered that subsequent knowledge concerning the intrinsic existence of phenomena, will be definitively ascertained and, consequently, recognized as authentic.

The enormous importance of direct engagement and the subsequent identification of the essential significance of phenomena, lies in the implication of cognitive autonomy. This liberty of cognition is unachievable through the intellect and unattainable through belief systems and imaginative mystical practices that alleges secret access to knowledge. Cognitive freedom is founded upon the immediate experience of the condition of reality by the human, essential ipseity. Therefore, it concerns the full, dimensional volume of existence.

We already reside within a world of intangible significances. We experience them continuously but fail to grasp their greater implication. The incorporeal, unique individuality of the human being is able to recognize those essentials and discern their greater implication. That is to say, the human self directly engages phenomena and is thereby able to discover the similarly essential distinction and significance of all things.

21. ARTICULATING INTANGIBLE REALITIES
Art as the Language of Quintessential Knowledge

Artistically, authentic, intangible realities are sometimes inadvertently articulated through trial-and-error. The artist subliminally senses a quality and struggles to portray it. But that which is articulated will not possess objective merit unless the intrinsic condition of the subject is discovered through a direct encounter of the essential human significance. Thereafter, the artist will be able to portray the authentic condition of an intangible situation through the language of a particular, artistic medium.

Additionally, there are levels of artistic skill that vary enormously. Some artistic expressions are merely exercises in composition more akin to craft. They may not necessarily articulate an intangible significance at all but remain merely pleasing to the eye through excellent craftsmanship.

The noblest assignment of art in the service of humanity is the communication of that which is essentially extant but which remains otherwise unrecognized through conventional cognition. Art is a means whereby the authentic conditions of existence may be revealed that otherwise have no voice. Art can show that of reality which would otherwise remain elusive because the intellect is unable to assess it and subjective perception is unable to categorically authenticate the intrinsic existence of a subject.

The neglected, elusive dimension of existence is composed of intangible, quintessential significances. These are the elemental condition of the existence of things, the intrinsic significance that distinguishes one person from another and the merit and value of phenomena. Furthermore, the qualitative condition that characterizes an organism or the conceptual paradigm of the archetype and the elusive nature of corruption and of virtue, all exist essentially yet incorporeally but they can be portrayed artistically.

If intangible existence is only vaguely experienced, then the articulation of physically elusive significances will appear as muddled and indecisive as our subjective appreciation of them. Consequently, the profound, authentic identities of phenomena tend to be disregarded in favor of tangible superficialities. That is to say, one can meet another individual superficially, merely according to their appearance or substantially according to who they are. The former is the materialistic approach whereby, ostensibly everything is evaluated in terms of the obvious. In reality no one really considers only the physical properties. We typically meet and attempt to assess the substantial identity of the other because the appearance alone is an inadequate perspective and unrealistic as a practical basis for a human relationship.

It is the intangible existence of a phenomenon that is significant because it is intrinsic and profound. In other words, it is the singular distinctiveness of a thing that is of interest and not merely the blatant, physical properties. However, that singularity is incorporeal and, as such, requires a different means of representation than material objects that can be readily described in physical terms.

The particular and unique identity of an object is that which is recognized when the essential, human singularity immediately confronts it. This directly experienced knowledge may then be described through the skill of an artistic medium. Consequently, true art is metaphoric, figurative and non-literal because the intangible identity cannot be literally depicted if it is entirely without physical form. This means that ssentials are not revealed through a terminology that portrays quantities and describes physical properties but by expressions that are ideally suited to describing qualities.

Authentic art is the language of qualitative significances. The vernacular of an artistic medium must be thoroughly mastered in order that the realizations of immediate experience and cognition may be represented with integrity. Art of such a caliber is justifiably attributed to genius both in terms of the acute knowledge directly ascertained through an immediate experience of incorporeal reality, and the skill and proficiency required in order accurately articulate it.

Art is the ideal language of intrinsic reality that is unrecognizable through conventional cognition. That is, qualities, values and essential identities cannot be logically thought-out but must be experientially recognized in order to be known. Intellectual scrutiny, sentiment and belief are the substance of conventional, human cognition but the qualitative is entirely unrepresented without the language of art and cannot be otherwise communicated. Without artistic portrayal, knowledge of essential realities remains an unarticulated, personal event.

There exists a confusion, typical of our time, whereby an art counterfeit, representative of self-indulgent expression or attractive composition without content, is acclaimed as meaningful. This is easily perceived and addressed when it is recognized that art is a skilled communication of a specific, intangible content and if either of these aspects is lacking, the classification of a work, as art, remains unjustified.

Art and craft, or the work of the artist and the artisan, have similarly become virtually synonymous in meaning. Art must articulate an otherwise intangible content. But craft is not a language or the communication device of a qualitative content but the pleasing production of something of usage. Similarly, tasteful composition, attractive collage and decoration remain craft if they do not intentionally reveal an intangible content and effectively portray it. Both art and craft are subjected to the same aesthetic necessity in that both strive to fabricate something through a wholesome and vivid composition but the goal of the one is to articulate an intangible essential while for the other content is not an issue.

Craft is not a language but it nevertheless demands technical skill. But art requires competence and dexterity of expression in order to accurately articulate a content that would otherwise remain elusive.

The beauty of an artistic expression is the integrity whereby the intangible content is communicated. Words, for example, are chosen for their figurative value in order to best articulate something that is not otherwise, readily describable through conventional means. Consequently, metaphorical speech is required in order to represent a content that cannot be explained precisely and strictly. But the literal language of the manual is appropriate to a description of the tangible, yet inadequate when it comes to qualities. Something beyond physical existence cannot be described literally but must be described figuratively.

In other words, art attempts to express qualitative realities that are incomprehensible to reasoning and indecipherable through logic. While intangible realities may be experienced directly, without the eloquent expression of an art language, they remain personal but otherwise suppressed.

Art can communicate the knowledgeable experience of intangible realities known through direct encounter by the authentic, human self. The particular content may be corroborated for its authenticity through a similarly straightforward experience of the particular artwork by the observer. Art can directly reveal authentic, incorporeal sublimities that confound intellectual abstraction.

Art is a privileged and complex skill of conversation that serves as a window of exposition for qualitative essentials. The inherent condition of incorporeal existence is revealed through genuine art work. Consequently, art is the noblest witness of quintessential significances that otherwise would remain ambiguous.

Beautiful poetry and music is reduced to monotonous automation when intellectual, logical thinking seeks to circumscribe it. Intellectually, the qualitative must be quantified in order to be logically assimilated. Thus, music is reduced to numerical values and poetry to structural analysis and meter. Distilled, quantitatively reduced properties do not even remotely articulate the sublime quality of a symphony because to the degree that the language of art is reduced and quantified, it also becomes an increasingly remote and meaningless articulation.

Much contemporary art, encountered through immediate experience is recognized to have degenerated into a self-indulgent expression whereby the artist attempts to reveal a subjective, emotional condition or to merely express and wallow in a personal event. It may even articulate a fiction or delusion. This is easily recognizable if the content is competently articulated and skillfully communicated. However, a content of such a nature will offer little of didactic value. Similarly, a poorly articulated missive will require a lengthy introduction proportionate to the lack of clarity and accuracy of its presentation.

While the self-indulgent artist, having mastered an art language, may accurately verbalize an emotional perspective and while the exploration may have personal therapeutic value and be skillfully communicated, it will remain of value only to psychological scholarship, as subjective art but fail in terms of substantive value.

The masterful use of the language of a particular artistic medium in the portrayal of universal qualities requires no explanation or introduction. The content will be eloquently articulated and elucidated as a communication discernible through the immediate experience of the viewer. The essential, intangible meaning will be recognized by the essential of the human being, the individual mind-self, in much the same way as the essential nature of all phenomena is similarly recognized. This is because the essential, human singularity similarly exists as an intangible significance.

The intellectual materialist insists that physical properties alone reveal the authentic nature of a phenomenon and qualities are somehow merely a subjective nuance. This absurd conclusion is ridiculed even by subjective commonsense and common acumen. But art tells us of the qualitative and our human, cognitive capacity of immediate experience and concomitant knowledge recognizes its profound authenticity.

Art is the means whereby essential realities once they are personally experienced and acknowledged, may be communicated. Therefore, the noblest practice of art, to deserve that designation, must involve the language of a particular, mastered medium through which authentic, intrinsic identities otherwise unrecognized, may be made known. That is to say, immediately apprehended significances require the lofty integrity and discipline of art in order to be fittingly articulated and communicated.

CONCLUSION

The distinction between our conventional thinking as an abstract, associative and emotive activity, and direct cognition as an experience of the intrinsic condition of things is not at first recognized as valid. However, it is clarified when one examines the way in which we usually think. Typically, our consideration of a phenomenon relies on our various memories of what we have known before. These preconceptions appear sufficient in most situations but nevertheless they are indirect assessments of the phenomena because they rely on prior evaluations. Similarly, we refer to our preferences and sentiments concerning a thing and consider it from the perspective of our liking or distaste. In this way, the usual evaluation of a thing is revealed to be essentially inadequate.

Our most reliable, conventional practice of cognition involves rationale. To the degree that deduction is ordered and disciplined, we arrive at moderately appropriate conclusions. But we have come to view phenomena exclusively in terms that are most suitable to our reasoning activity. Our scientific approach has taught us to examine data derived significantly from physical properties. Consequently, the circle is complete when we entirely discount all experiential knowledge and deem only the material aspects as valid. Neglected are the intangible qualities and a contrived world-view is established composed exclusively of dead matter in various physical arrangements.

Qualities are experientially known by every human being and therein lies the inherent contradiction between the contrived explanation of life that consists solely of material properties and that which is directly experienced. Unfortunately, the philosophy of the materialist has gained the whole-hearted support of the scientific community because it similarly deals exclusively with physical properties. Thereupon, a certain monopoly of understanding has been granted to deductive reasoning even though authentic, familiar qualities are incommensurate with the physical and consequently disregarded. Through this approach a very distorted perspective has developed towards life that is exclusively materialistic. Even the religious community scarcely competes with the authority of physical, analytical deduction but because a dogma must rely on faith and it is itself contradictory in its conclusions and interpretations.

The most pressing need is for the individual is to assert an autonomy of thought that is independent of external authority The monopoly on truth assumed by both the materialist and religious authority will then be abandoned by the individual in favor of knowledge that is discerned through direct cognition.

The immediate volume of meaningfulness that we discover through direct cognition is neither abstract nor the exclusive domain of an elite leadership. Therefore, through straightforward engagement we begin to recognize that what we are directly experiencing is the authentic while our former manner of thinking is of little value when it comes to definitive knowledge. Furthermore, we realize that reality exists independently without human assistance or interpretation and that things have a more profound significance that is intrinsic.

When we inhibit our conventional thinking

practices we directly discover what a phenomenon is through immediate experience, and thereby we discern the independent, substantive nature of its existence. That is to say, we want to know what a thing is essentially and intrinsically and what it is of itself, and to do that we must engage the phenomenon impartially and directly without the usual, conceptual interference.

Experiencing something directly and in present timing reveals the inadequacy of our conventional thinking in determining the intrinsic and characteristic nature of things. The practice of cognition whereby the authentic identity of something is determined, suggests a far more extensive reality than that gleaned from mere appearances. Therefore, if we wish to know what things essentially are, we can do so through the inherent, human capacity of direct cognition. But we cannot allow intangible significances to be subsumed by a materialistic approach which denies validation to anything that is unmanageable to the analytical and appraising intellect. The essential condition of things is intangible and cannot be assessed unless it is confronted directly and experientially by the similarly essential human entity.

A phenomenon must be experienced through an open-minded approach as if the object has never been considered before and is assumed unknown to us through the name or description. Therefore, we begin afresh from a perspective that assumes we know nothing concerning it. We want to know what it is without tainting it with our preconceptions because our inquiry is concerned with the intrinsic identity, and it is that which we wish to ascertain. Consequently, we are disinterested in an appraisal founded upon the superficial, physical properties or the appearance but we need to know the quiddity and inherent identity of the existence of the phenomenon.

We realize that every phenomenon is intrinsically identifiable, and it occurs to us that there is a whole intangible volume composed of elusive qualities and values. Therefore, imagination is set aside, and we cease to wonder what something is as we turn our attention to the essential distinction and recognize its imminent significance. We observe immediately, in present timing, through the consciousness of our own authentic individuality. In other words, the ipseity that we determine as our own intrinsic, human identity is of the same substance as the essential distinction of the object under examination. Thereupon, the profound singularity is directly experienced, and we superimpose nothing upon it in order that we may obtain direct knowledge concerning its inherent identity. Therefore, we come to know something for what it actually is.

Clearly there are two practices of human cognition. The one deals with how a thing works while the other identifies what it is. The analysis of physical properties encourages a technology that is exclusively material but direct cognition involves the knowledge of what things intrinsically are. Intrinsic distinctions are intangible. Through knowledge of the authentic nature of something the human being becomes familiar with the essential identity and can compare that quality to other circumstances and determine if they ring true.

The difference between the two cognitive practices lies in the recognition of a substantial, yet incorporeal proportion of existence and one that is merely material without the subtlety of qualitative nuances. This awareness includes our own human identity as well as the capacity to discover the essential of other things.

In other words, this cognitive liberty involves immediately ascertained knowledge of what things authentically are. But immediate engagement also requires the recognition of our own authentic condition of existence whereby, between the two, the human being becomes emancipated from a deadening, myopic perspective.

There is nothing mysterious or mystical about the practice of direct cognition. It is merely unfamiliar. Abstract thinking founded upon preconceptions and deduction is readily preferred over the effort and discipline that immediate cognition requires. But the conclusions of indirect assessment will always remain unsatisfactory to us through their obliqueness and insufficiency because remotely thinking about things is hardly comparable in quality to direct knowledge and the experience of imminent existence.

Assuming no prior knowledge allows the adjunct faculty of the authentic, human identity to immediately engage the condition in which the authentic nature of things resides. Once experienced nothing less than directly engaged reality will suffice.

Ultimately, reason implies the evaluation of information dependent upon indirectly ascertained data. It is an intellectual activity removed from direct experience. However, the exploration of the human faculty of direct cognition is self-perpetuating because experiential knowledge of the intrinsic identity of ourselves and of the phenomenal world as it exists essentially, enables and enhances wisdom. Furthermore, familiarity with the actual reveals speculation and fabrication for what they are. Things are identified in terms of their authenticity or lack of it because we have direct experience of the tenor of intrinsic knowledge and we know what profound and meaningful existence is reality like.

In other words, we come to realize through the practice of direct cognition that when indirect or abstract thinking is postponed, we contemplate things immediately and we recognize that every phenomenal thing, of itself, is composed of intangible, intrinsic significance.

Other Books by the Same Author

TOWARDS A MEANINGFUL FUTURE
The Continuum of the Qualitative Expansion of the Soul

THE IMMANENT PRINCIPLE OF INTEGRITY AND GOODWILL
The Integration of the Principle of Virtue within the Human heart

THE EVOLUTIONARY IMPERATIVE OF OUR TIME
The Crucial Establishment of an Inspired Ethos with the Individual, Human Heart, appropriate to a Meaningful Future

RECONCILIATION WITH HUMAN DESTINY
The Surrender of the Heart-of-the-Soul as the Expedient Approach Towards Direct Engagement with the Immanent Exemplar of a Future, Human Disposition

THE QUALITATIVE EVOLUTION OF THE SOUL
The Evolutionary Transformation of the Human Soul Through Openhearted Sincerity Towards Immanent Caritas

THE SUPERNAL ETHOS
Unanimity with the Divine Nature

THE BEGINNING OF WISDOM
Knowledge through Immediate Engagement

UNDER THE AEGIS OF IMMANENT CARITAS
The Reorientation of the Human, Disparate Self-circumscribed Mentality

THE DECEPTION OF MATERIALISTIC WESTERN PHILOSOPHY
An Exploration of the Physically Elusive Volume of Existence

THE MEANINGFUL VOLUME OF EXISTENCE
An Exploration of the Overlooked Intangible Significance of Phenomena

THE OBSOLETE SELF
Individual Uniqueness and Significance beyond Egocentrism

HUMAN SOVEREIGN AUTONOMY
The Discovery of the Human Ipseity and its Establishment as the Essential Authority of the Human Constitution

THE TRANSFORMATION OF THE SOUL
From Self-centeredness to Sovereign Autonomy

THE IMPLICATION OF HUMAN INCORPOREAL EXISTENCE
The Overlooked Significance of the Intangible and Qualitative Dimension of Existence

IMMEDIATE EXPERIENTIAL COGNITION
The Inherent Human Capacity of Immediate Engagement

THE HUMAN ESSENTIAL IDENTITY
Direct Experience of the Intangible Significance of Existence through the Immediate Engagement of the Human Essence

www.ingramcontent.com/pod-product-compliance
Lightning Source LLC
Chambersburg PA
CBHW061255110426
42742CB00012BA/1928